D0896233

10 Minutes to Live

Surviving an Active Shooter Using A.L.I.V.E.®

PRAISE FOR
10 MINUTES TO LIVE

"**This is one of the most concise and professional books I have read on active shooters.** Easy to read and understand, this book is excellent and straight to the point on ways for any individual to take action and provide for their own safety."

— *Amazon Customer and Reader*

"**A compelling and uplifting read**. This is a different twist to the DHS 'Run, Hide, Fight' philosophy, developed by a seasoned practitioner. This was put together in an easy to read, easy to follow format. Well done, Michael!"

— ANTHONY TIEGER, *California*

"**This book could very well save your life.** Well written and thoughtful. You clearly understand what you need to do to have a chance. I highly recommend every parent read this book."

— LIZ, *Reader, Student and Parent, Illinois*

"Sadly, I purchased this book the day before yet another mass shooting at a public school unfolded. **Mr. Julian has laid out a straight forward and practical method for surviving. I can already see from reading this book and the news reports, how more lives could have been saved had the victims practiced what this author lays out here**. I plan on carrying this book with me on vacations, business trips and to large gatherings."

— *Amazon Customer and Reader, California*

"Thank you, Michael. **Clearly written for those who perhaps may need a small nudge of encouragement to do or say the right thing in the face of danger, this may just be the inspirational tipping point they need**. Well done, sir!"

— EUGENE F. FERRARO, *Security Consultant, Colorado*

"No one is too young or old, strong or weak, to follow the advice in this book. No special training - just a very strong mindset. **Every school administrator, teacher, student, and parent should have this book as required reading at every grade.** The evil that people will do to themselves and each other is never a surprise – it is a dark reality."

— CHRIS STORY, *Trainer, Investigator, Consultant, U.S.A.*

"Excellent read and right on target. **It is a must read for Security and Police Professionals.**"

— DEAN A. BEERS, *Professional Investigator, U.S.A.*

"A very good read in explaining how to survive an active shooter/active threat situation for the novice. Having years of experience from the military, law enforcement and now Executive Protection, I found that Mr. Julian breaks down the information in an easy to read and understand fashion. It will open the reader's eyes to be more situationally aware. **With all of [the] past decades of mass threat incidents, I highly recommend this book. It may just save your life.**"

— RICHARD MARRUFFO, *Security Consultant*

"**A truly inspirational read for folks of all ages and from all walks of life.** Mike's simple writing style reaches to the depths of our inner fears and then elevates us with the notion we are all capable of great and heroic acts of courage when others need us the most."

— RICHARD CORONA , *Retired Banker, Connecticut*

"**Great book. Very well written and easy to read.** Fantastic information and really hits home. I also highly recommend the Surviving an Active Shooter Course taught by Mr. Julian!"

— BARBARA WRIGHT, *Amazon Customer and Reader*

"**Well written & concise. I would recommend to anyone interested in learning more about this topic.**"

— JAMES HAMILTON, *Security Consultant, California*

10 Minutes to Live

Surviving an Active Shooter Using A.L.I.V.E.®

MICHAEL JULIAN, CPI, PPS, CSP

BCG Publishing

10 Minutes to Live
Surviving an Active Shooter Using A.L.I.V.E.

Publisher:
BCG Publishing

Second Edition,

Names: Julian, Michael, author.
Title: 10 Minutes to Live : Surviving an Active Shooter Using A.L.I.V.E. / Michael Julian.
Description: 2nd edition. | Murrieta, CA : Michael Julian, 2018. | Includes bibliographical references. | Also available in ebook and audio format.
Identifiers: LCCN 2017917485 | ISBN 978-0-692-99219-7 (paperback)
Subjects: LCSH: Mass shootings. | School shootings. | Survival. | Self-defense. | Self-preservation. | BISAC: REFERENCE / Survival & Emergency Preparedness. | SOCIAL SCIENCE / Violence in Society.
Classification: LCC HV6536.5.U6 J85 2019 (print) | LCC HV6536.5.U6 (ebook) | DDC 613.6/6--dc23.

International Standard Book Numbers:

ISBN-13: 978-1-957255-01-9 (Paperback)

Cover design by Michael Julian

DEDICATION

I dedicate this book to my father, Ron Julian, without whom I would likely never have learned so much about security and investigations or have been pointed in the direction of a career in these professions.

To my two children, Michael and Alexandra, without whom I would never have felt a sense of purpose higher than myself and would never have learned the true value of life.

And to my incredibly competent executive staff—because of their professionalism, skill, and dedication to running my companies, I had time to write this book.

Courage is not living without fear. Courage
is being scared to death and doing the right thing at the
right moment in spite of fear.

—Michael Julian

CONTENTS

FOREWORD

Congratulations, reader! The mere fact that you are reading this book means you have already taken the first and most critical step in protecting yourself and those around you. That critical first step, of course, is personal responsibility! You have made it your responsibility to do whatever is necessary to not only survive but also prevail over those who wish to inflict VIOLENCE upon innocents.

Unfortunately, because of cultural changes and the untethered growth in government institutions and regulations during the last 50 years, the concept of "personal responsibility" and its true meaning have become watered down to mean "personal reliance"—a reliance on those institutions and agencies (be they municipal, state, or federal) to keep us safe. In the truest sense, we have become reliant upon institutions rather than ourselves.

The author has given you a well-researched and common-sense road map to do what is not only necessary but also mandatory for those subjected to the horror of an active shooter who wish to survive to go home and be with those they love.

Having had 32 years' experience in law enforcement and counterterrorism investigations at the federal level, as well as experience as a tactical-response-team commander, I can attest to the statement, "When seconds matter, the police are only minutes away!" It will be up to you!

Thomas "Mac" McCaffrey
Senior Special Agent (Ret.)
United Stated Department of the Treasury

DISCLAIMER

While I have made every effort to properly research, credit, and cite the material referenced herein, in numerous instances it was impossible. Where it was possible, I noted the identity of the likely or most probable source. However, where that was not possible or the task was simply too difficult, I noted such if I thought doing so would benefit the reader. If by chance someone else was first to record those words, I apologize. If informed of such, I will give credit where due in the next edition.

It is understood that neither I nor my publisher are qualified or licensed to provide legal advice. As such, together and individually we disclaim any notion or appearance of such. If you are in need of legal advice, carefully search and find a lawyer. Goodness knows there are enough of them.

Critics will likely notice that I seem to prefer the male gender when writing. This is due, as of the date of this writing, to the fact that more than 97% of active killers in history were male. However, please do not allow my style or choice of pronouns to distract you. What is important is that your life or that of a colleague, friend, or family member might depend on what you learn from this book.

On a final note, the reader should know that this book was written so as to be read cover to cover. However it has been formatted so any reader, at any time, can merely open the book and read it and learn. Occasionally I have sprinkled true-life short stories here and there where I thought you may relate.

The stories, however, are not intended to entertain. Each story carefully reveals a lesson. Make the best use of them and prepare to learn!

—Michael Julian, CPI, PPS, CSP, Murrieta, California

INTRODUCTION

This book is intended to change minds and persuade. While other books on the topic of surviving an active shooter event are intended to inform, I have specifically set out to convince you that the opportunity to survive is not just luck or chance, it can be a choice. This book will reveal how to save your life or that of someone you know. No longer need we be victims. It is time each of us becomes a survivor!

For all intents and purposes, the first edition of this book was complete and headed to print when, on October 1, 2017, millionaire businessman Stephen Paddock opened fire on the audience of the Route 91 Harvest Country Music Festival from the 30-second floor of the Mandalay Bay Hotel and Casino in Las Vegas, Nevada. In doing so he killed 58 people and wounded over 500 more, then killed himself before police breached his guest room door.

This was the deadliest active shooter event in modern American history and the first mass shooting from a highly elevated position since August 1, 1966, when Charles Whitman opened fire on campus from the 27th floor observation deck of the Clock Tower at the University of Texas in Austin.

So, I pulled the book from print because I felt it imperative I address this event and lend some thoughts on how to survive future events like these.

There is very little one can do while standing shoulder to shoulder in a crowd of thousands of people when an active shooter opens fire from above. However there are things you can and should do to increase your chance of survival. When entering a large venue such as the open-air location of a music festival, take note of your surroundings.

Pause, look around, and force yourself to be situationally aware. Now carefully consider the following:

1. Ask yourself (and remember) where the entrances and exits of the perimeter of the park, amphitheater, or concert hall are located.

2. Make a mental note of the entrances and exits of the interior of the venue, including vending areas that may have a back door through which you can escape.

3. Look above you. Identify potential locations or perches from which a shooter can fire and attack.

4. Position yourself for safety. Many attendees purchase the closest to the stage, most centrally located seats possible to better enjoy the show. However, sitting or standing near an exit increases your ability to LEAVE quickly and safely. Additionally, sitting or standing near a pillar, wall, or solid barrier makes it possible to take cover once the origin of the attack is determined.

Many people have never even heard a gunshot except for a Hollywood sound effect on television. Now that the footage of the Las Vegas incident has been broadcast on every news network, and the video has gone viral on all social media sites, people have heard what real gunfire sounds like. React immediately when you hear that sound. Immediately warn those with you and *respond appropriately*. Your life may depend on how quickly you react.

Then, only five weeks after *Las Vegas*, on Sunday, November 5, another horrifying mass killing occurred, taking the lives of 26 people, including children, while they worshipped at the First Baptist Church in Sutherland Springs, Texas. The shooter, 26-year-old Devin Kelley, a dishonorably discharged Air Force service member with a history of violence against family members and animals, entered the church and began randomly shooting.

It has been speculated that these murders were not religiously motivated, and that domestic violence was the catalyst because the killer's estranged wife and her family were regular parishioners at the church. Hearing the sound of gunfire, a nearby resident, Stephen Willeford, armed with a rifle, engaged the shooter and took chase when Kelley fled the scene in his waiting SUV. Having been shot and seriously wounded by the armed citizen, the killer called his father, telling him that he did not believe he would make it. After losing control of his vehicle and crashing, he shot himself and ended his life.

I've since had the opportunity to become friends with Mr. Willeford after interviewing him on my podcast. His heroic and selfless actions that day became apparent as he told me the story of how yelling to Kelley from outside the church, stopped his shooting rampage and drew him outside, where he engaged and shot him six times as Kelley entered his vehicle to flee. I believe we can all feel safer knowing that sheepdogs like Mr. Willeford walk among us.

What is the victim to do? What would you do to protect yourself and your loved ones next to you when a madman attacks? When you are staring into the eyes of a killer whose only goal is to take your life, what can you do to survive? Without a weapon or a plan, your immediate actions or inactions may determine your fate and the fate of those around you. But what if you were part of a team, using the A.L.I.V.E. training to take down and neutralize the assailant? *You have a duty to yourself and those who love and depend on you to use these five simple survival steps to stay A.L.I.V.E.*

ASSESS

When a killer opens fire in a crowded area, the resulting body count will depend on how quickly the intended victims react. In that split second when your brain acknowledges what is happening, you must ASSESS the situation in an instant and decide, based on where the gunman is and your available options, what to do next: *LEAVE, IMPEDE the killer's ability to harm you, or use VIOLENCE against them.*

LEAVE

If you are near an exit and can escape with your loved ones without drawing fire from the shooter, stay low and run as fast and as far away from the incident as possible, not stopping until you are too far away to be harmed. Call 911 immediately upon realizing what is happening.

IMPEDE

If able, take cover behind something solid, or if possible, step into a side room where you can lock and/or block the door. Don't hesitate, do it immediately, leaving your belongings behind. If your only option is to drop to the ground, do so.

Take whatever cover is possible and avoid bringing attention to yourself and those around you. In this step your objective is to create TIME and SPACE.

VIOLENCE

Whoever is closest to the shooter must act. With VIOLENCE, he or she must attack the threat with the intent to kill. If a gunman is pointing the weapon to his left, the person(s) closest to him on his right must attack with all their might. Or if you are not immediately close to the shooter, but his gun jams or he runs out of ammunition and must reload, if you believe you can get to him before he completes his reload, do whatever it takes, with anything available, to make it impossible for the gunman to continue firing. You must commit to the commission of complete and total VIOLENCE upon the assailant. If you do not seize the opportunity if availed, you and the people around you may die.

EXPOSE

Once the shooting has stopped, EXPOSE your position carefully. The gunman may have moved on, may have become disarmed or disabled, or may simply be reloading. He may be alive and injured but still a threat. There will be chaos, people screaming, crying, and begging for help. Confusion may be all around you. If you expose yourself too early you may endanger your life and those nearest you.

Having the proper *security* mindset prior to and a *survival* mindset when such an event begins will dramatically increase your chances of survival. Being situationally aware—taking note of exits and barriers to use as cover and sitting or standing near them when possible—should always be considered.

Your purpose, your mission, and your single objective…is to *stay A.L.I.V.E.*

CHAPTER ONE

IT WASN'T ALWAYS LIKE THIS

KEY LEARNING POINTS:

1. Lessons we've learned from the killers at Columbine and the significance of how that tragedy and others like it have affected our everyday life and sense of public safety.
2. These killers often telegraph their intentions with behavior that, when taught to recognize, we can take averting action to stop the outcome.
3. The *ability to survive* an active shooter may come down to a choice, and *only you* can make that choice.
4. Immediate action against the killers, when possible, can save countless lives.

I had the pleasure of providing a full day of instruction at a beautiful location on the West Coast, where my client and host was a well-known global technology company and my students were a collection of male and female employees, most of whom were 40 and under. The audience was a mixture of new hires and tenured employees as well as members of every level of management, including the organization's CEO. They were engaged and very interested in hearing what I had to offer.

Among the many questions I was asked during the day, one struck me as particularly insightful. Confidently, a youngish-looking man stood and politely asked, *"Has our world—our schools and our workplaces—always been this dangerous?"* As is typical in many tech companies, during open forums, group meetings, and lectures, attendees enthusiastically applaud when a particularly interesting or controversial question is posed to the speaker. Once the applause subsided enough for me to respond, I gave a simple *NO*. No, our world, our schools, and our workplaces have not always been this dangerous, nor need they be.

Depending upon one's age, personal experience, and recollection of the past, the demarcation point when that change occurred varies significantly. However, among those who have studied the subject we today call *active shooters*, and those who eat and breathe survival (such as myself), the point of change is clearly Columbine. Other than armed conflicts, few events in our history prior to 9/11 touched so many and so deeply, and changed the way we think and act, in striving toward ensuring our safety and survival of a violent event.[1]

Ground Zero

The Columbine High School massacre was a school shooting and attempted bombing that occurred on April 20, 1999, at Columbine High School in Littleton, Colorado, United States. The perpetrators, both twelfth grade students (Eric Harris and Dylan Klebold), murdered 12 students and one teacher, all of whom were killed by gunfire. Ten students were killed in the library, where the pair subsequently committed suicide. At the time, it was the deadliest recorded shooting at a school in United States history, not surpassed until 2012 by the Sandy Hook Elementary School shooting, where 28 people (mostly children) were murdered. But the Colorado massacre inspired copycats, and *Columbine* has become a byword for a school shooting and, in general, an active shooter event.

The two perpetrators injured 21 additional people with gunshots and also exchanged gunfire with the police. In fact, the first shot fired by the killers was directed at one of the school's resource officers who saw them enter the school. In the mayhem that ensued, another three people were injured trying to exit the school.

In addition to the shootings, the attack involved several homemade improvised explosive devices (IEDs). The largest of these were placed in the cafeteria, powerful enough to kill or seriously injure all students present at the busiest lunch hour and possibly even collapse the second floor, crushing anyone who may have survived the explosion. They planned to shoot and toss bombs at the injured and survivors still able to flee. However, IEDs failed to detonate. Car bombs were also placed in the parking lot, and a bomb was placed at another location away from the school, all of which were intended to kill and divert first responders. These bombs, too, failed to detonate.

The pair planned the massacre for at least a year and wished for the massacre to rival the Oklahoma City bombing and cause the most deaths in United States history. *USA Today* referred to the attack as "planned as a grand, if badly implemented, terrorist bombing."

Because of existing protocols and operating procedures at the time, police were slow to enter the school and were heavily criticized for not intervening during the shooting. The incident resulted in the introduction of the *Immediate Action Rapid Deployment* tactic, which is used in situations where an active shooter is trying to kill people rather than take hostages. Columbine also resulted in an increased emphasis on school security and the introduction of the idea of what became *gun-free zones*. Debates were sparked over gun control laws and gun culture, high school cliques, subcultures, and bullying. Also debated in the aftermath were the moral panic over goths, social outcasts, the use of pharmaceutical antidepressants by teenagers, teenage Internet use and violence in video games, movies, and our culture.

Harris and Klebold also used their schoolwork to foreshadow the massacre. They both displayed themes of violence in their creative writing projects. Harris wrote a paper on school shootings, and a poem from the perspective of a bullet. Klebold wrote a short story about a man killing students, which worried his teacher so much that she alerted his parents, to no avail. Both had actively researched war and murder. For one project, Harris wrote a paper on the Nazis and Klebold wrote a paper on Charles Manson. In a psychology class, Harris wrote he dreamed of going on a shooting spree with Klebold. Harris's journals described several experimental bombs the two built and tested. The pair had telegraphed violent intentions going back two years in writings, videos, online posts, and conversations with and in front of friends, some of whom faced criminal charges after the fact for helping them acquire firearms and lying to law enforcement about their knowledge of the pending attack.

Once inside the school the attack unfolded. As shots rang out, inside the school cafeteria teacher Dave Sanders and two custodians, Jon Curtis and Jay Gallatine, initially told students to get under the tables. After realizing such antiquated training was not effective in that type of situation, they then successfully evacuated almost all of the students up the staircase leading to the school's second floor. The stairs were located around the corner from the library and school's main South Hallway. Hastily, Sanders tried to warn as many students and teachers as possible. However, Harris and Klebold were now roaming the hallways looking for targets. In passing the library, Sanders gestured for students to shelter in place.

Then joined by another student, Sanders and the student encountered Harris and Klebold face-to-face. Spontaneously, Sanders and the student turned and ran in the opposite direction. Harris and Klebold opened fire, hitting Sanders in both the back and neck but missing the student. Klebold walked toward Sanders, who had collapsed as a result of his wounds, stepped over him, tossed a pipe bomb down the hall in the opposite direction, then casually returned to Harris's side to walk up the North Hallway toward the library.

Sanders, once alone on hands and knees, struggled toward the science area, where another teacher assisted him into a classroom with 30 students that had taken cover there. First aid-trained, student Aaron Hancey attempted to stop Sanders's bleeding for three hours. While waiting for help, and in spite of student Deidra Kucera posting a sign in the classroom's exterior window reading, *1 BLEEDING TO DEATH*, Sanders slowly bled to death.

At exactly 11:29 a.m. the killers entered the school's main library and began to kill. First taunting the cowering students and demanding the "jocks" to identify themselves, the killers methodically killed as many as they could easily find there before returning to the cafeteria.

Before taking their own lives in the cafeteria, the Columbine killers had fired a total of 188 rounds of ammunition. Harris had fired nearly twice as much as Klebold, a total of 96 shots with his carbine rifle, and discharged his shotgun 25 times. Klebold fired the TEC-9 handgun 55 times, and 12 rounds from his double-barreled shotgun. Law enforcement officers fired 141 rounds during exchanges of gunfire with the killers, but not a single round is known to have hit either of the murderers.

So while guns were used as the implements of death, it is easier to blame the guns than the people who used them. Were it only that simple. Experts on the psychology of killing have stated that bullying, social isolation, psychosis, substance abuse, narcotics, video games, the Internet, and violent videos and movies containing gratuitous violence all played a role. But what is most clear is that active killers are willing to die if it enables them to kill first. Guns appear to be merely a tool of convenience.

Two of the many school shootings that have taken place since Columbine illustrate the need for immediate action when no other options exist.

On May 7, 2019, 18-year-old Devon Erickson and 16-year-old Maya McKinney entered the STEM Charter School in Highlands Ranch, CO. When Erickson entered a classroom and pulled a gun, a young hero, Kendrick Ray Castillo, along with two other students, too close to Erickson to run away or take cover, jumped on Erickson to prevent him from systematically executing students one by one. Castillo was shot and killed during the encounter, but had he done nothing, he and the other students would have been shot anyway with little or no chance of survival. Because of his and the other two students' immediate and selfless response, multiple lives were saved.

Another tragic but clear representation of immediate aggression toward an active assailant saving lives took place on April 30, 2019 at the University of North Carolina at Charlotte, when Trystan Andrew Terrell rushed into a classroom and opened fire. Student Riley Howell tackled the shooter while yelling, "Go, Go, Go!" to the other students. Howell was shot and died of his injuries but saved the lives of several classmates rather than freezing in fear and waiting to die.

What Did We Learn?

So what did we learn from Columbine and the seemingly innumerable horrors since? While the lessons are many, fundamentally we have discovered:

1. Active killers have one goal: to kill as many people as possible in as little time as possible.

2. Once we realize the violence is in the form of an active killer, we now know what our next steps must be, understanding their intent.

3. These killers, as many did after them, sought vengeance (power and control) upon others for what they felt were injustices against them.

4. Active killers telegraph their actions long before the event and could have been anticipated. This type of violence is a process, not just an event.

5. Indecision or freezing in fear is the worst possible thing you can do to survive.

6. Simply hiding under tables in a catastrophic event, as many were taught in school as children, is not an effective survival method against active shooters.

7. If in the path of an attack, put obstacles between you and the killer (create time and space), take cover, and/or conceal your location to IMPEDE them.

8. When no other option exists because the event unfolds immediately and right in front of you, you may have to commit VIOLENCE against your assailant to stop them using any means necessary.

Thus, one of the principle purposes of this book is to assist you to learn from the past and help you better prepare yourself, your employees, your coworkers, and even your families and friends so that if you ever find yourself in the *path of an attack*, you will know precisely what to do to increase your chances of survival. You will be the one who goes home that night to love, hug, and kiss your family once again.

When I give my classes on active killers and how to best survive them using the A.L.I.V.E. (which stands for ASSESS, LEAVE, IMPEDE, VIOLENCE, and EXPOSE) Active Shooter Survival Program, about 50% of the time, I have an attendee who says that he or she doesn't know what an active shooter/killer is. So let's make sure you know exactly what I'm talking about when I use these terms.

Active Shooter/Killer/Assailant Defined

The term *active shooter* is one we've probably heard the most in the media, as many mass killings do involve some type of handgun or long gun (usually both), and many media outlets find more sensationalism in events that involve firearms. However, I often use the terms *active shooter, active killer,* and *active assailant* interchangeably, as sometimes the weapon of choice isn't a firearm. It's a knife, sword, bat, explosives, or some other object capable of inflicting great bodily harm and death on many people in a short amount of time. Since the first edition of this book was published I've begun using *active assailant* (the label many in the international security community have moved toward as a catch-all for this type of behavior) in my A.L.I.V.E. presentations and online training courses, and have added it in several places in this new edition. So, what is an active shooter/killer/assailant, exactly?

The definition of an active shooter/killer/assailant is someone whose intent is to kill three or more people, usually in a confined area, and generally in places where there are a lot of people to kill in as little time as possible (like movie theaters, workplaces, event centers, places of worship, and other areas where people congregate in larger numbers), and there is typically no pattern or method to their selection of victims. Essentially, the more lives lost, the more people who die during the event, the more "successful" the active killer feels.

Undoubtedly, some of what you're about to learn is going to be completely disturbing. It's shocking, really. But I want you to think about this as an opportunity to take positive, proactive action that could someday save your life or the lives of your coworkers, family, and friends. Here's your chance to learn something that could empower you survive one of the most chaotic and terroristic events imaginable, so you can continue to live your life, pursue your dreams, and attain you goals.

During my in-person trainings, I show several videos of recorded attacks. They give the viewers a front-row seat to what it would be like to be there, so it's not uncommon to hear some of the attendees say, "I didn't like the videos, but I'm glad I saw them because now I know what it's really like. Now it's real to me." They feel better prepared because they're taking the class. That's how I want you to feel when you finish this book.

Why You Shouldn't Go Another Day Without Knowing This Material

I purposely wrote this book using as few words as I could while still creating as great an impact as possible because I want it to be a quick and effective read, without fluff that would bore you and prevent you from finishing this lesson. There are many reinforcing stories, anecdotes, quotations from other books, and other information I could have inserted to qualify the information herein. But as someone with a short attention span myself, I know how easy it is to get distracted and move on to something else, which would defeat my purpose in creating this simple lifesaving message.

I often relate my message directly to those who hire me to teach their employees how to survive an active shooter event, but this book is written for everyone. It applies to work, home, social, and spiritual locations, so whenever I speak to anyone in this book, know that I am speaking to you.

Did you know that when an active shooter opens fire, on average, nearly a dozen innocent people are injured and killed? Look around your workplace or some of the areas you frequent where there is a moderate number of people. How would you feel if three of them lost their lives? And how would you feel, knowing that another nine or so would be lying in agony if an active assailant arrived right now?

Imagine, too, if you were one of them. What if you were the one lying on the ground shot or stabbed? What if you were the one who was senselessly attacked, even though you may never have done the perpetrator an ounce of harm?

Being prepared for events like these is the best possible tool for survival. Knowing what to expect, as well as knowing the actions you can take to keep yourself as safe as possible, is critical for you, your family, employees, coworkers, customers, and the public. It may be fire, tornado, or earthquake. We all know that these things happen, so the more we're ready for them when they do, the better our chances of survival. The same is true with active killers. These events occur, and they're happening more often, so the more we know how to respond when they do, the greater the likelihood that we won't become one of the innocent victims whose picture is splashed across the evening news.

For example, if an unstable employee, ex-employee, or employee's family member entered your workplace with a weapon right this moment, would you know what to do? If a current or former student of your high school or university came on campus and began shooting, do you know the correct physical and psychological responses to dramatically improve your chances of survival? These are serious questions that every safety manager, human resources supervisor, risk management professional, employee, caretaker, teacher, student, and parent should be able to confidently answer YES!

No one wants to think an active killer will enter his or her workplace, school, house of worship, theater, grocery store, shopping mall, medical facility, etc. but the fact is that it could happen anywhere and, perhaps most disturbingly, it seems to be happening with increased frequency. Massacres like the one that occurred at the Inland Regional Center in San Bernardino, California, where an employee left a holiday party and returned shortly after, killing 14 and injuring 17 others, are becoming an all-too-familiar scenario facing our workplaces and our world.

This means that people can no longer subscribe to the notion that "it will never happen here," especially given the frequency and severity of workplace attacks. In fact, that way of thinking is extremely dangerous, which is why I've dedicated an entire chapter of this book to changing that way of thinking. Too many people are injured or killed in these types of attacks because they walked into them with the mindset that "it will never happen to me."

It's Time to Open Your Eyes and Train for These Events

Now is the time to adequately and effectively train yourself, your family members, coworkers, and staff how to best respond to an active killer attack, giving you all a fighting chance. Not after something has happened or during an attack, but now. Now is the time to teach everyone what they need to do to best mitigate their risk of injury and death should an active killer strike.

The longer you're able to stay alive in an active killer incident, the better your chance of surviving the entire event. And I'm not talking about having to fight for your life for hours either. As you'll soon learn, if you can survive the first 10 minutes of the attack, then you have greatly increased the odds that you'll survive the incident.

In the pages ahead, you'll discover how to do the following:

- Identify behaviors, causes, and red flags typically associated with nonrandom workplace violence and active killer incidents before they occur.

- Develop enhanced situational awareness and a security mindset, making you a less attractive and "harder" target for an active killer.

- Train everyone around you to assure that each person knows how to safely and effectively respond to an active killer event with a survival mindset, giving you a stronger team.

- Take what you learn and put it into action, with training scenarios for you to practice both in and out of the workplace.

Sheep, Wolves, and Sheepdogs

Dr. Dave Grossman, Psy.D., a retired US Army Lieutenant Colonel, former Professor of Psychology at the US Military Academy at West Point, creator of the Killology Research Group, and incredibly pragmatic speaker, is the author of such books as *On Killing, On Combat, Assassination Generation, Warrior Mindset, Bulletproof Mind*, and *Sheepdogs*. In his writings, he tells a story of the concept of the sheep, the wolf, and the sheepdog. Though many people give Col. Grossman credit for creating this concept, he explains that he learned it from a "Vietnam veteran, an old retired colonel" who said:

Most of the people in our society are sheep. They are kind, gentle, productive creatures who can only hurt one another by accident.

Then there are the wolves and the wolves feed on the sheep without mercy.

Then there are sheepdogs and I'm a sheepdog. I live to protect the flock and confront the wolf.

Grossman paraphrases this ideology by stating, "If you have no capacity for violence, then you are a healthy productive citizen: a sheep. If you have a capacity for violence and no empathy for your fellow citizens, then you have defined an aggressive sociopath—a wolf. But what if you have a capacity for violence, and a deep love for your fellow citizens? Then you are a sheepdog, a warrior, someone who is walking the hero's path. Someone who can walk into the heart of darkness, into the universal human phobia, and walk out unscathed."

I want you, the reader, to keep this concept in mind as you consider what I teach you in the coming chapters. Think about this concept and imagine where the players (i.e., perpetrators, victims, and heroes) fit into this ideology, and where you fit, or should fit, when you apply "proactive reactionism," as will be discussed in Chapter 5. Think about which one you would be, as a natural reaction to a violent event, and which one you should be. It will become all too clear how your mindset can and will dramatically affect your chances of surviving an active shooter event.

A Passion for Your Safety

So why am I so passionate about this topic? What do I know about active killer scenarios that could possibly help you survive if you're ever in one?

I've been involved in the investigations and security industries my entire life. My dad, Ron Julian, started our parent company, National Business Investigations, Inc. (NBI), in Fullerton, California in 1967. Then, in 2003, I founded MPS Security & Protection as the security division to offer our clients even more safety and security-related services.

As the president and CEO, I'm ultimately responsible for conducting vulnerability assessments, assisting with risk mitigation, teaching effective workplace violence prevention, and providing executive and asset protection services for my clients. I use the knowledge and skills I've learned during my training at the Executive Protection Institute in Winchester, Virginia; the Behavioral Threat Assessment and Active Shooter training offered by the Department of Homeland Security; and Covert Surveillance and Surveillance Detection from Executive Security International in Grand Junction, Colorado, where I learned about protective and counter surveillance. I pass my knowledge and skills along to others so that fewer innocent lives are shattered or lost when an active killer decides to strike.

These areas are my passion. They're my excitement. They're what I love to do. That's why, with NBI running efficiently and effectively because of an amazing administrative team, I'm moving more into the educational space, spending a majority of my time teaching people about active shooters and how to survive them. I do this by sharing the A.L.I.V.E. Active Shooter Survival Program, something I've developed and trademarked to help close the gaps I've found in other training programs I've observed, knowing that someday it will save lives. Who knows? It may even be your life that will be saved, solely because you took the time to prepare yourself and those around you. If that's the case, then I've done my job. I've served my purpose. But understand this: whether it's my program or someone else's, the important thing is that you learn how to do something, anything, in the event you find yourself face-to-face with a person whose only goal is to take your life.

Theodore Roosevelt said, "In any moment of decision, the best thing you can do is the right thing, the next best thing is the wrong thing, and the worst thing you can do, is nothing." In an active shooter situation, considering a shooter's goal of taking as many lives in as little time as possible, truly the worst thing you can do is nothing because you will become a statistic.

As you will read in Chapters 3 and 4, I refer to the importance of your mindset, of knowing the mindset of the person intending to do you harm, and of having the correct mindset to survive when you are faced with that situation. But first, let's start with addressing the wrong mindset, which you may have already. This begins with talking about the "it won't happen to me" mindset. So if you've ever thought that, this first chapter is dedicated to you.

---

[1] Columbine occurred before the 9/11 attack, which began with a pair of hijacked airliners intentionally flown into the New York World Trade Center towers.

CHAPTER TWO

IT WON'T HAPPEN TO ME

KEY LEARNING POINTS:

1. The danger and life-threatening consequence of *optimism bias* and how to avoid it.
2. *No place is immune* from an active shooter event. There's no day or time of day that is safe from an active shooter who intends to kill.
3. Active shooter events can happen anywhere, and the number of active shooter events is increasing each year.
4. Other than being male, *there is no major common characteristic of active killers*, therefore, other than recognizing behavioral signs of potential violence, profiling is impossible.
5. Admit that being faced with an active killer is a possibility and create a response plan.

Turn on the news after an active-shooting incident, and one of the first things you'll likely see is a reporter interviewing someone who was at the scene, possibly even one of the victims. Inevitably, at some point during the conversation, the interviewee almost always says, "I knew things like this happened, but I never thought it'd happen to me." Why are we so blind to the fact that this type of event not only can happen to everyday citizens, to the good people in this world, but it does?[2]

Dr. Richard Osbaldiston, Ph.D., associate professor at Eastern Kentucky University, calls this way of thinking, *optimism bias*. Specifically, he defines it as holding "the belief that each of us is more likely to experience good outcomes and less likely to experience bad outcomes," causing us to "disregard the reality of an overall situation because we think we are excluded from the potential negative effects".

Put simply, believing that it won't happen to you requires the false belief that you're somehow immune to the bad things that happen in this world. Not only is this way of thinking wrong, it's extremely dangerous.

The Danger Associated with This Belief

Do you think that the people who went to see a movie at the Cinemark Century 16 theater in Aurora, Colorado on July 20, 2012, ever thought they'd find themselves face to face with a gunman by the name of James Holmes? Or what about the holiday shoppers who went to Clackamas Town Center in Portland, Oregon on December 11, 2012, intent on buying Christmas gifts for their loved ones, expected to endure chaos and terror as a gunman meandered through the mall picking out targets?

While optimism bias is common, Dr. Osbaldiston points out that this way of thinking prevents people from heeding warnings associated with known risks, making it a dangerous way to live because we fail to see the threat until it's right in front of us and may be too late to avoid. It's like being told that carrying excess body weight elevates your risk of diabetes, heart disease, and a host of other potentially life-threatening conditions but disregarding this information and being surprised when diagnosed with a disease.

Several research studies have been conducted on optimism bias and have found that it is relatively widespread. One such study was published by *Health Psychology* and involved four different pieces of research performed on college students. Each one set out to ascertain the students' thoughts and perceptions regarding risk, and after reviewing the results, the researcher concluded that, overall, the university-level participants' views "were overly optimistic" and failed to acknowledge the real risks they faced.

In the case of active assailant incidents specifically, those who enter these types of situations with their blinders on, completely unprepared and disbelieving of the possibility that a person with a weapon could present immediate harm, have just moments to respond and to respond appropriately. So if they're caught off guard by the prospect of even being in this circumstance, they waste valuable seconds trying to come to terms with what's evolving around them. Not to mention that the worst time to formulate a plan is when you're in the middle of a crisis and are unable to think clearly and rationally.

Active Shooter Incidents Can (and Do) Happen All the Time, Everywhere

To change this mentality and get rid of the "it won't happen to me" belief that is so dangerous to hold, it's important to acknowledge the fact that active killer scenarios happen all the time. This begins with educating yourself about how often these incidents occur.

According to the Federal Bureau of Investigation's (FBI) 2021 report examining 20 years of events, there were 333 active shooter incidents, causing 2,851 casualties between January 1, 2000, and December 31st, 2019. Do the math, and you realize that's roughly 1.4 active shooter events causing nearly 12 casualties every 30 days.

In fact, if you look at the FBI's data you'll notice a disturbing upward trend. During the first seven years of this time frame, an average of 6.4 incidents occurred annually. This number almost tripled during the next seven years and quadrupled over the following six years, with roughly 28 incidents per year during the last three years.

This report also examines where in the continental United States these events have occurred. Of the 50 states and District of Columbia, active killings have taken place in 47 states during that 20-year span, the highest number occurring in California, Florida, Texas, and Pennsylvania.

Realistically, the true number of active shooter cases is likely much higher. Google alerts are e-mailed to me anytime this type of incident occurs and I usually receive notifications four to five times per week. However, because some incidents don't always fit neatly into the government's active shooter definition, they're not counted as such, which means they happen much more frequently than they appear in the news.

Take the shooting on April 10, 2017, at North Park Elementary School in San Bernardino, California for instance. Cedric Anderson went to the school that day intent on killing his estranged wife, yet he also shot two students while he was there. Was he an active shooter? Yes. But not all agencies would classify this as an active shooter incident, excluding it from their data and failing to capture just how often these types of incidents occur.

Look more in depth at the individual incidents, and you also learn that these deadly scenarios can happen anywhere. Below is an updated breakdown from an FBI study of 333 active shooter events covering 20 years, with 2,851 casualties, from the beginning of 2000 to the end of 2019.[3]

- 148 in <u>businesses</u> (107 open to the public, including 10 at malls, and 41 closed to the public) – 1,042 casualties. That's more incidents than the next four categories combined.
- 62 at <u>educational</u> environments including pre-K-12 up to higher education – 419 casualties
- 21 occurred on <u>governmental</u> properties – 89 casualties
- 9 on <u>military</u> properties – 106 casualties
- 15 occurred at <u>healthcare</u> facilities 62 casualties
- 15 occurred in <u>houses of worship</u> – 147 casualties

- 50 in <u>open spaces</u> – 895 casualties
- 13 occurred at individual <u>residences</u> – 89 casualties
- 1 was categorized as "other"

Review the list again and you'll quickly realize that 2/3 of active shooter incidents take place in the workplace and schools. For those occurring in the workplace, while a disgruntled employee would seem more likely the cause, the reality is that three out of every four shooters are not an employee or former employee of that organization, which is all the more reason to be prepared for anything with training like A.L.I.V.E.

Active shooters don't necessarily stay in one location either. In more than 15% of the cases, the shooter spreads terror and chaos to multiple locations. Sadly, these types of "roaming active killers" will likely increase over time.

So, are there any locations that don't fit into at least one of these categories? No, which is why it's so important to realize that there's no place you can go and be 100% safe from an active shooter. Even police departments, buildings that should be the safest place there is, aren't immune to active shooters, as evidenced by the shooting at the McKinney Public Safety building in which a gunman sent more than a hundred rounds directly toward the headquarters.[4] Even a military office is vulnerable, such as when, on July 16, 2015, Muhammad Youssuf Abdulazeez opened fire on two military installations in Chattanooga, Tennessee. He first committed a drive-by shooting at a recruiting center, then traveled to a US Navy Reserve center and continued firing, where he was killed by police in a gunfight. Four Marines died on the spot. A US Navy sailor, a marine recruiter, and a police officer were wounded. The sailor died from his injuries two days later.

If you're stuck on the numbers, certain that they're wrong because you don't remember hearing about these mass killings, you're not alone. Sure, some of these active shooter cases are well-known. The Virginia Tech shooting on April 16, 2007, for example. In this case, Seung-Hui Cho went to the school, located in Blacksburg, Virginia, with two handguns, chained the doors shut, and started shooting for 10 minutes, eventually killing 32 people and wounding 17 more. That case was all over the news for months.

The shooting at the Cinemark Century 16 in Aurora, Colorado, on July 20, 2012, was also well publicized. Images of James Eagan Holmes were continuously flashed across television screens, declaring that this mass murderer with distinctive red hair went to this movie theater with multiple firearms, killing 12 and wounding 58 by the time he was done. Experts probed into his personal history with great fervor, looking for every possible sign that should've alerted the people in Holmes's life that he was capable of this type of mass casualty and talking about it endlessly on air.

Not All Cases Make National News

Most active shooter incidents aren't as well remembered because they either don't quite make it to the national news or, if they do, they aren't covered long enough to make a big impact . One example is the September 22, 2010, active shooter incident that occurred at AmeriCold Logistics in Crete,

Nebraska. Just before 10:00 a.m., Akouch Kashoual entered the workplace and started firing at his coworkers, wounding three. Luckily, all victims survived, but this incident could easily have gone the other way, especially if Kashoual hadn't decided to take his own life before law enforcement could arrive on the scene (a circumstance that is common, by the way, for reasons we'll go into later).

A more recent example occurred on May 29, 2016, beginning in an auto detail shop before the shooter, Dionisio Garza III, took his rifle into a nearby residential area. By the time this incident was over, one innocent person had died and six more had sustained wounds (two of whom were law enforcement personnel).

Again, no place is immune from an active shooter incident. There's no time of day that is exempt from these killings either. Some of these incidences have happened at 2:00 a.m. (like the June 12, 2016, shooting at the Pulse Nightclub), and some have occurred in the middle of the afternoon (such as the June 5, 2014, shooting at Seattle Pacific University).

This Way of Thinking Is Negligent

The point of providing these statistics is not to frighten you (although it should); they are intended to get you to see that having an *it won't happen to me* mentality is not only foolish but also negligent—dangerously negligent.

You owe it to yourself and to your family, friends, coworkers, and everyone else around you to understand and acknowledge the dangers that exist in this world. To pretend they don't exist puts everyone—you and them both—in harm's way.

To keep your eyes closed to this reality is like closing your eyes to the fact that children are curious by nature and can easily find themselves in the bathroom cabinet, taking one of the many medications that are there. Leave childproof locks off the doors, and you're inviting trouble; and if you do find yourself in a predicament where your child ingests one of these harmful substances, you may be delayed in providing an efficient, life-saving response simply because you never considered this scenario a possibility.

Don't put yourself, your employees, your family, or your friends in this situation with active killers because you're too scared to admit that you may someday find yourself in a scenario that involves a person actively shooting at you or those around you. Instead, admit that it's a possibility, and then do the one thing you can do today to increase your chances of survival, as well as the chances of those around you: create a response plan, at least in your mind for personal benefit, if not on paper for your family and/or organization.

When making this plan (and regularly and consistently training with the plan you've created), keep in mind that it's your response during the first 10 minutes of an active assailant incident that matter most.

---

[2] R. Osbaldiston, *It Won't Happen to Me: The Optimism Bias*, March 2, 2016.

[3] "Active Shooter Incidents 20-Year Review, 2000-2019," Federal Bureau of Investigation, https://www.fbi.gov/file-repository/active-shooter-incidents-20-year-review-2000-2019-060121.pdf/view.

[4] F. Heinz, "Man Fires More than 100 Rounds at Police Headquarters," NBC 5, August 7, 2010, http://www.nbcdfw.com/news/local/Shots-Fired-Outside-McKinney-Police-Station-100886034.html.

CHAPTER THREE

WHY THE FIRST 10 MINUTES MATTER MOST

KEY LEARNING POINTS:

1. The majority of active shooter events involving mass casualties span 10 minutes or less, most lasting less than five minutes.
2. One cannot rely solely on law enforcement arriving in time to stop an active shooter. It's likely that those being targeted must play a critical role in saving their own lives.
3. Even unarmed citizens can end the threat.
4. *If you can survive the first 10 minutes* of an active shooter event, *you are likely to survive the attack*, regardless of its duration.

I n 2014, the FBI conducted a study on the 160 documented active shooter incidents that occurred between the years of 2000 and 2013. One of the primary purposes of this research was to learn more about these types of situations, so government officials could be more proactive in preventing them from occurring in the future.

But the FBI had a secondary goal as well. It also wanted to create a more effective and faster law enforcement response, should an active shooter present himself at one of our nation's schools, retail businesses, event gatherings, or any other location that could easily result in mass casualties. Too many people were dying in the time it was taking police to arrive on scene and take control of the situation.

Therefore, part of this study involved calculating the amount of time that elapsed from the time the shooter began inflicting violence on innocent bystanders until the threat (the shooter) was neutralized. The results?

Out of the 160 active shooter situations that occurred during this 13-year time frame, the exact duration of the incidents could only be determined in 63 of the scenarios. However, of these 63, the incident had come to an end in five minutes or less, more than two-thirds, or 69.8%, of the time.

As if this weren't bad enough—five minutes is hardly enough time to formulate a response, let alone enact it—some incidents didn't even last that long. In fact, in 36.5% of the cases in which the duration could be ascertained, the incident was over within a mere two minutes, or about the same amount of time it took you to read up to this point in this chapter.

10 Minutes to Live

Most active shooter incidents that resulted in higher numbers of mass casualties have still reportedly ended within 10 minutes. Here are a few of the most well-known events that have occurred in recent history that meet this criterion:

- **Virginia Tech shooting, April 16, 2007**

  The killer shot two people at West Ambler Hall at 7:15 a.m. The second attack, which now fell into the definition of an active shooting, occurred at 9:42 a.m., when the gunman killed 32 students and teachers and wounded 17. Approximately 10 minutes after he began, the killer committed suicide..

- **Fort Hood shooting, November 5, 2009**

  From beginning to end, this shooting lasted only 10 minutes. In that time, 12 service members and one US Department of Defense employee lost their lives.

- **Sandy Hook Elementary School shooting, December 14, 2012**

  The first shot was fired through the plate-glass window of this Newtown, Connecticut, school just after 9:30 a.m. Between that time and 9:40 a.m., which is when the gunman turned his firearm on himself, 20 first graders and six school staff members sustained life-ending injuries.[5]

In all three of these cases, the active shooter incident lasted only 10 minutes. While we all know how long 10 minutes is, realization doesn't often set in as to exactly how fast this amount of time goes by until you start thinking about the things you do that take approximately 10 minutes' time.

What Can You Do in 10 Minutes?

If you're an average person, 10 minutes is about how long it takes to fold a load of laundry, scrub the toilets, or vacuum a room in your home. Ten minutes is also roughly how much time you spend to read your child a book, make yourself a sandwich, put a roast and veggies in the crockpot for dinner, or compile your weekly grocery shopping list.

Now, imagine that while performing one of these actions, you must find a way to survive an active shooter scenario. Not much time to think about and implement an appropriate and potentially life-saving response if you haven't already thought about and planned for it, is it?

But wait. You will have police and other law enforcement personnel who can come to your aid and stop the active shooter, right? While the answer is yes, as most areas of the United States do have some type of contracted police coverage, but the officers likely won't appear as quickly as you need them to save your life before the event is over.

Police Response to Active Shooters

Case in point: an article published by *POLICE* magazine cited the Department of Homeland Security's finding that, for school shooters specifically, the average law enforcement response to these types of calls took 18 minutes. I believe this response time has become significantly shorter in recent years given our current knowledge of how vitally important it is to confront the shooter as soon as possible. But even if it was shortened by five minutes the police couldn't get on scene, find the assailant, stop the threat, and implement life-saving measures until roughly three minutes after shooting had already ceased.

With more and more budget cuts to governmental agencies, this issue is likely to get worse before it gets better. For instance, on February 21, 2017, Fox 5 in San Diego, California, ran a story about how budget cuts could cause the local schools to lose 21 officers. That's 21 fewer police personnel who could potentially save the lives of students and staff, leaving the entire district more vulnerable to an active shooter scenario.

In short, one cannot rely solely on law enforcement to stop an active shooter. Instead, it is up to all of us as individuals to do our part.

To be clear, this doesn't mean that you must always and immediately take on an active shooter one-on-one, placing your life in danger, nor should you if you can avoid it. But it does mean that it's your responsibility to know what you can do to better protect not only your own life but also the lives of those around you if you ever find yourself in the middle of this type of scenario and want to survive.

You Are Part of the Response

That's why this nation's top law enforcement agency suggests that you train for these types of scenarios. In their 2000 to 2013 study results, after reporting the finding that most active shooter incidents are over within a few minutes' time, the FBI stated:

Recognizing the increased active shooter threat and the swiftness with which active shooter incidents unfold, these study results support the importance of training and exercises—not only for law enforcement but also for citizens. It is important, too, that training and exercises include not only an understanding of the threats faced but also the risks and options available in active shooter incidents.

Basically, by regularly participating in exercises designed to mimic an active shooter incident, you will become more prepared to respond should you find yourself in this circumstance. It's not much different than practicing how you'd escape from your home in the event of a fire or how you'd respond should a major earthquake suddenly occur. The more you practice these types of scenarios, the more efficient your response.

Since most active shooter incidents end within 10 minutes or less, it becomes your response that mainly determines whether you (and those around you) survive. This is especially true as, regardless of how responsive the police are, arriving on scene before the incident is over is almost impossible unless the officer was on the property or in the area when the shooting began.

Stopping the Active Shooter

Upon hearing that one has a limited amount of time to formulate and implement a response, the next question is usually, "If you only have five to 10 minutes from the beginning of the incident to the end, exactly how do you stop an active shooter?"

While some active shooter situations are ended by the shooter committing suicide (which occurs in roughly 56% of the cases) or by some type of law enforcement response, in some of the cases, additional lives are saved by everyday people (sheepdogs) who are selfless and quick-acting enough to stop the shooter and the threat.

Specifically, in 13.1% of the cases studied by the FBI in 2014, it was an unarmed citizen who stepped in and ended the threat, creating a successful resolution. Half of these unarmed individuals were educators or students, which is no surprise due to the number of shootings in school-based settings during this time. The others were everyday people who happened to be in the area when the shooting began and decided to act to stop the threat.

It should be noted that in six additional cases, it was an armed person who stepped in and stopped the attack. Some were off-duty police officers or security guards. Others were citizens who were carrying a firearm. But what would have happened if those shootings had occurred in a weapon-free zone? Who would have been able to step in with equal or greater means then?

Of course, there are also the lives saved that can't be put into numbers. After all, there's no way of knowing how many more people the shooters would have taken out had their attacks not been stopped.

Plus, there are the lives that were saved solely because someone had the forethought to create some type of obstacle or barrier that prevented the shooter from reaching and subsequently injuring or killing more victims. This happens in cases where people have overturned tables to block doors or have hidden in a dark supply closet to give the appearance that the room was empty.

Using the 10 Minutes to Your Benefit

While it may seem like having a mere 10 minutes to respond could work against you, there's a major benefit to this short time frame. Primarily, if you can manage to survive for the first 10 minutes of an active killer incident, then you have a good chance of surviving the incident in its entirety.

Keep this in mind when practicing your own active shooter scenarios (whether mentally or physically), because what you do in this small time frame could likely determine whether you live or die. To better help you in your training, so you can make the situations and scenarios more realistic, the next chapter will explain what goes on inside the mind of an active shooter.

---

[5] "Gunman Kills Students and Adults at Newtown, Connecticut, Elementary School," History.com, accessed May 31, 2017, http://www.history.com/this-day-in-history/gunman-kills-students-and-adults-at-newtown-connecticut-elementary-school.

CHAPTER FOUR

WHO IS THE ACTIVE SHOOTER?

KEY LEARNING POINTS:

1. There is no demographic group exempt from becoming an active killer.
2. Though women have been known to participate in mass shootings, those *events with the largest number of casualties are attacks perpetrated by males.*
3. The overwhelming majority of events involving fatalities are committed by a single active shooter.
4. The principle weapon of choice of the active shooter is a *handgun.*
5. The *active shooter seeks ultimate control and power* and believes that unleashing terror with intent to kill provides him the ability to attain this goal.

While, according to the FBI study there are no demographic groups exempt from becoming an active killer, statistically speaking, there are certain qualities or traits that many past shooters have shared. The first is gender.

Male-Dominated Incidents

In the FBI's report identifying the 160 active shootings between 2000 and 2013, all of the incidents involved male shooters except for six committed by females. This male-dominated trend continued in 2014 and 2015, with 39 of the 42 active shooters in those two years being male and the remaining three females.

Because more men tend to be active shooters than women, it sometimes makes it difficult to think of or remember actual cases in which females were the perpetrators of mass casualty, but these cases do occur. For example, on September 8, 2016, it was reported that five shots were fired at Alpine High School in Alpine, Texas.[6] The shooter was a 14-year-old girl.

In another school-based shooting, this one occurring at Louisiana Technical College, it was also a female behind the gun's trigger. In this case, the 23-year-old woman reportedly killed two students and wounded 20 more before finally turning the gun on herself.[7]

And yet another on April 3, 2018, when 38-year-old Nasim Najafi Aghdam opened fire at YouTube headquarters in San Bruno, CA with a Smith & Wesson 9 mm semi-automatic pistol. Aghdam wounded three people, one of them critically, before killing herself.

Active Shooters by Age

The FBI's 20-year study further reinforced the percentages of the age groups of active killers we learned from previous studies. Here's a breakdown of the ages of the perpetrators in the shootings occurring from 2000 to 2019.

Of 345 events, 336 were ages 20 to 79 with nine unknown, pre-teen, or in their 80s.

Age Range	Number of Shooters
Teen	50
20-29	103
30-39	60
40-49	63
50-59	35
60-69	19
70-79	6
Unknown/pre-teen/80	9

They Typically Work Alone

According to the FBI, out of the 40 incidents between 2014 and 2015, an overwhelming majority (38 of them) involved one active shooter per scene. The remaining two were carried out by two shooters each: a husband and wife. And of the 160 active shooter events between 2000 and 2013, 98.9% of the killers acted alone. This indicates that most active shooters are solitary in this regard.

This isn't always the case, however. Take Columbine, for example. This incident involved two shooters: Eric Harris and

Dylan Klebold. So, while this type of situation doesn't happen as often as the sole shooter, it can still occur.[8]

Warning Signs

Certainly, none of these demographics on their own mean that someone will someday become an active shooter. However, there are a few common signs that could potentially indicate that someone is thinking about or possibly even planning a nonrandom act of violence. These include the following:

- aggressive or threatening behavior or remarks
- bizarre or irrational behavior, emotional outbursts
- sudden or extreme behavior changes
- unresolved relationship or family issues
- serious financial problems
- depression or untreated mental illness and personality/emotional disorders
- alcohol or drug abuse
- comments or threats related to suicide or homicide
- history of violence

Keep in mind that these alone aren't usually enough to send someone over the edge, but if there are other factors (other warning signs), the person in question could be triggered to commit an act of violence.

As an example, imagine that a person you work with starts to act differently. You find out they are going through a divorce, just found out their spouse is having an affair, or facing bankruptcy. As a result, that person becomes depressed and starts drinking. Enough emotional stress can cause most people to crack in one form or fashion. Fortunately, most people are not predisposed to acting out by way of mass casualty violence.

Active Shooter Triggers

Some of the time, the active shooter's trigger is work-related. Maybe the person was recently reprimanded, given a demotion at work, or forced to take a decrease in pay. Termination of employment can be a trigger as well, as can, and oftentimes has, having some type of dispute with a fellow employee or with someone in a supervisory role. If the person feels like the supervisor has marginalized or has it out for him or her, it could easily send them over the edge.

Other times the trigger is personal. This is evidenced by the FBI's report that 10% of active shooter incidents are initiated with the killing of a family member. Personal situations that could serve as a catalyst for this type of event include having relationship issues like going through a divorce, enduring a child custody battle, having a child in trouble with the law, or any number of other incidents involving stress within the family unit.

Financial issues can act as a trigger as well. This is particularly relevant for men because, historically, in our society men are supposed to be the providers, to take care of their family's financial needs. When they can't, when they're forced to deal with bankruptcies, home foreclosures, or car repossessions, some simply snap. As more women are becoming the primary or equal bread winners in our modern culture, we may begin to see more active killer events carried out by women who are faced with financial challenges.

Weapons of Choice

When we talk about the active shooter, it's pretty much implied that the shooter has some type of firearm, thanks largely to the media perpetuating the term "active shooter." As shown by the FBI 20-year study, whether involving a handgun or a long gun (344 used handguns, 144 used long guns, and 58 used shotguns), most incidents are carried out with a weapon that fires a projectile. But sometimes mass killings occur with other types of weapons.

For example, edged weapons like knives and machetes have been used in the past to inflict mass bodily harm. Here are a few incidents to consider domestically and abroad:

- In 2017, a 16-year-old New York boy stabbed four other teens as a continuation of an in-school fight.

- Four women who were identified as members of a separatist group attacked multiple innocent bystanders at a Chinese train station in 2014, ultimately killing 29 of them and causing injury to 130 others using only knives.

- Twenty-two children and one adult were stabbed in a seemingly motiveless 2012 knife attack at one Chinese school.

- A 37-year-old janitor with a knife killed six boys and two girls (all first or second graders) and injured 15 more in a Japanese school in 2001, and that was after previously being arrested for accusations of "spiking the tea of four teachers" at a school in 1999.[9]

- An Australian woman who was said to suffer from "severe schizophrenia" brutally stabbed and killed all seven of her children (four sons and three daughters) and a niece in 2014.

- In 2015, nine alleged Uyghur separatists killed 50 sleeping workers in a knife attack that took place at a Chinese coal mine.

- Five hundred Nigerians in three different villages died at the hands of attackers with machetes in 2010 solely because they were Christian.

- In 2008, Steve Kwon attacked and killed his ex-wife, her boyfriend, her two children, and another male with a samurai sword and a bat in Quartz Hill, California.[10]

Other weapons used in mass killings include explosives and explosive devices. For instance, on May 18, 1927, 38 students and 6 adults were killed at Bath Consolidated School in Bath, Michigan, when more than a thousand pounds of dynamite exploded. The reason for the blast? The killer, Andrew Kehoe, was upset about school-related property taxes.

In April, 2021 I was retained to present my in-person A.L.I.V.E. training to a group just four miles from where the Bath School once stood. Since getting the lifesaving method of A.L.I.V.E. to as many people as I possibly can has become my life's work, I could not pass up the opportunity to see the actual place I had studied in my research for this book. With very little time before my flight home was to depart, I drove my rental car (possibly bending the local speed laws) to the site of the Bath School and stood on the very spot those 44 innocent people died

This type of mass casualty event is even more prevalent internationally. In 2015, 22 people were killed and 120 were injured when a three-kilogram pipe bomb was detonated at a Bangkok shrine.[11]

Gasoline and matches have created their fair share of damage too. In 1990, 87 people were killed at a social club that Julio Gonzalez had set on fire after having been thrown out because he was arguing with his former girlfriend. This caused the victims to be "trapped screaming and crying in the dark."

Even sarin gas has been used as a mass killing strategy. In 1995, 12 were killed and an additional 5,500 people required treatment after 10 terrorists associated with a religious cult released sarin gas in a Tokyo subway.

Mass casualty can result from other objects too. For instance, in September 1911, one man entered two separate Colorado Springs homes and killed all six occupants with the blunt end of an axe. (The fact that some of these incidents occurred in the early 1900s is proof that mass killings are not an entirely new phenomenon.)

It's also not uncommon for active killers to use more than one weapon in an attack. One piece of research conducted by the *Washington Post* found, after reviewing 130 such incidents, "shooters brought an average of four weapons to each shooting; one carried seven guns." What can drive people to this point?

Three Primary Motives

The reasons that some people decide to go on mass killing sprees can all be boiled down to three main motives: anger/revenge, mental illness or personality/emotional disorder, and ideological.

Anger or Revenge

If something happens that causes a person to feel angry, he or she may decide to get revenge via an active shooting. Causes of this anger could include job termination, having conflict with someone, or dealing with financial and/or personal relationship issues. Having been bullied, humiliated, or marginalized could also elicit this response if, in their mind, the person sees violence as the solution to the issue because they believe others are to blame. One example of a revenge-type shooting occurred in a Bay District school board meeting in Panama City, Florida; the incident was captured entirely on video, which I show in my training.

When the meeting was opened to public comment so citizens could voice their concerns, 56-year-old Clay Duke got up, spray-painted a red V in a circle on the wall, and then kicked all of the spectators out, leaving only the board members in the room. They had no choice but to listen to Duke express his anger at the fact that his wife (who had previously worked for the district) had been fired, causing financial issues, all while he continued to wave a gun.

After moments of some back-and-forth conversation and comments, Duke aimed directly at superintendent Bill Husfelt and fired. This was followed by several shots fired at the other board members as well. It was then that Mike Jones, a retired police officer and the school's chief of security, entered the room and shot and wounded Duke, who fell to the ground. Duke then committed suicide with his own gun.

Duke wanted revenge on the school board for what he felt "they'd done" to his wife and ultimately to him. In his eyes, they were to blame for the way his life had taken a downward spiral, so they became the target of his retribution.

Mental Illness or Personality/Emotional Disorder

Have you ever looked at a picture of someone who committed a mass killing? James Eagan Holmes for instance, who dressed in tactical clothing, set off teargas grenades, and shot into the audience with multiple firearms inside a Century 16 movie theater in Aurora, Colorado, during a midnight screening of the film *The Dark Knight Rises*. Or Adam Lanza, the active killer at Sandy Hook Elementary in Newtown, Connecticut, who caused the death of 20 first graders and six school staff in 2012? Could you see in their eyes that something was amiss? This often happens in cases in which mental illness or personality/emotional disorder is the underlying cause of the random act of violence.

The National Alliance on Mental Illness (NAMI) reports that one out of every five (or 43.8 million) Americans suffer from some type of mental illness or personality disorder per year. Additionally, 18.1% of these types of disorders involve anxiety, 6.9% involve depression, 2.6% involve bipolar disorder, and 1.1% involve schizophrenia. Certainly, most people with mental disorders don't strive to kill masses of people, but sometimes these mental conditions are a contributing factor.

The Virginia Tech shooter Seung-Hui Cho, for instance. Prior to killing 32 people and wounding 17 others on April 16, 2007, Cho created a pre-shooting videotape confession in which he said, "I did it. I had to." He also took 29 different photos of himself in a wide array of positions, many of which involved him pointing a gun directly at the camera. It was later discovered that Cho's medical records revealed a history of mental health issues; Cho had even been admitted to a psychiatric ward in 2005 after his roommate said that he had threatened suicide.[12]

Ideological Reasons

Some active shooters commit these violent acts with the intention of creating fear within the population, what we commonly refer to as "terror," based on a cause that they care or feel deeply about. Sometimes the cause is political, sometimes it's religious or racial, or sometimes it's something completely different in which the person is still extremely passionate.

An example of extreme religion-based mass killings in modern times are the murders attributed to ISIS, the Islamic State in Iraq and Syria. On July 16, 2016, the *New York Times* published data from a self-conducted analysis indicating that more than 1,200 people outside Iraq and Syria have died at the hands of ISIS, almost half of whom were Westerners. Of course, that doesn't include the time 2,977 people were killed by another radical Islamic group, Al Qaeda, in the 9/11 attacks (2,753 of whom were on one of the hijacked planes or in the twin towers, 184 of whom died when the plane crashed into the Pentagon, and 40 of whom were passengers and crew members killed when their plane crashed into a Pennsylvania field).

Ideological reasons were also behind the 2009 mass killing committed at Fort Hood by US Army Psychiatrist, Major Nidal Malik Hasan. Based on reports, it's said that Hasan shouted "Allahu Akbar"—which translates to "God is great" in Arabic—before killing one Department of Defense employee and 12 service members.

An example of an active killer whose racial ideology was the foundation of his ruthless acts is Dylann Roof, a 21-year-old self-proclaimed white supremacist, who, on June 17, 2015, initiated a mass shooting against an all-black congregation at Emanuel African Methodist Episcopal Church in downtown Charleston, South Carolina, with the hope of starting a race war. After killing nine people and injuring one other, he escaped but was apprehended a short while later and was ultimately convicted and sentenced to death.

It's All About Control

In the end, whether the incident is initiated due to anger, revenge, ideology, mental illness, or criminal behavior, the primary driving factor behind active shooter incidents is typically control. This control gives shooters the sense of power they long for after feeling powerless to change the factors or events in their lives that have brought them to this point.

Shooters are attempting to take charge when it feels like they don't have any control, or need more control, over what is occurring in their lives. You see this all the time in cases in which shooters have been previously bullied by student peers or supervisors, were belittled for their beliefs, were rejected by their wives, or were otherwise in situations that they couldn't change or rectify rationally.

The active shooter knows that engaging in this type of event gives them ultimate control, ultimate power. They control others via fear and the taking of their lives. They also gain (or regain) control over their own lives. Some in my industry call this the "God complex." You will read many times over the course of this book that the primary goal of active killers is to kill as many people as possible in as short a time as possible because they know that the end will come, so they need to achieve their goal quickly.

This desire and elation for finally regaining the control and power the killer feels he deserves, but in their mind was taken from them, is so strong they will take their own life rather than lose that power to someone else taking their life. That is why it is so important to get law enforcement on the scene as soon as possible; the killer will frequently kill themselves just at the possibility that police are there and close enough to rob them of that final ultimate power. To them, even in death they will have the last possible element of control because they killed themselves before someone else could do it. They controlled their own fate to the very end.

As you will see at the end of this book in the chronological list of active killers who took their own lives between the years 2000 and 2017, many of the killers committed suicide before or just as law enforcement arrived rather than be taken alive or killed by someone else. This section illustrates how frequently they would rather kill themselves than lose the sense of control and power they have, in their minds, regained from their horrible deeds.

The exception to this, however, are those who kill in the name of Islam. Radical Muslims believe they will live forever in "Paradise" if they die while advancing or defending the name of Allah and the religion of Islam. Escaping to fight again or fighting to the death is their preferred conclusion, as witnessed during and after the Inland Regional Center killings in San Bernardino, California.

And of course, in the eyes of the killers, the best way to enhance getting the control they always wanted is to keep the control after the event by letting the world know who they are and that they have control. Many active shooters, such as Elliot Rodger in Santa Barbara and Seung-Hui Cho at Virginia Tech, knew their story would be publicized, allowing that control to last even beyond their death. Those two and others went as far as creating videos of themselves describing what they would do prior to their killing spree, so the media could perpetuate their brutal acts long after they were gone. Unfortunately, this has given would-be killers a study guide to plan future attacks; they now know their stories will live on long past their demise.

What They Fear and What They Don't

Active shooters don't generally fear death. Yes, they may fear dying at the hands of another because it takes control away from them, but they usually have no fear of death itself. In fact, if you've ever seen a recorded active shooter incident, you may have noticed the shooter had a tremendous sense of calm before and during the attack. This is because they felt in control. It's bizarre and hard to comprehend as a normal-thinking person, but all witness accounts speak to that.

The one thing the active shooter *does* fear is not accomplishing his or her goal of killing as many people as possible in as short amount of time as possible. That's why they're intent on taking out as many people as they can as quickly as they can. To be stopped short would mean they didn't do what they set out to do; it would mean they lost control. They lost that feeling of power they so desperately sought.

So how do you deal with individuals with this type of faulty mindset, with these "wolves"? It all begins with creating the right mindset yourself: a survival mindset.

[6] "At Least 1 Student Shot at Texas High School, Female Shooter Dead," Fox News, September 8, 2016, http://www.foxnews.com/us/2016/09/08/shots-fired-at-texas-high-school-at-least-one-person-injured.html.

[7] Associated Press, "Woman Kills 2 Students in Louisiana College Classroom, Takes Own Life," Fox News, February 8, 2008, http://www.foxnews.com/story/2008/02/08/woman-kills-2-students-in-louisiana-college-classroom-takes-own-life.html.

[8] For more statistics on this topic see Appendix B or visit: "Active Shooter Incidents in the United States in 2014 and 2015," FBI, accessed December 9, 2017, https://www.fbi.gov/file-repository/activeshooterincidentsus_2014-2015.pdf/view.

[9] K. Hall, "Knife-Wielding Attacker Kills Eight, Injures 15 at Japanese School," *Lubbock Avalanche Journal,* June 8, 2001, http://lubbockonline.com/stories/060801/upd_075-3395.shtml#.WTwkLIWcGUk.

[10] A. Myers, "Man Pleads Guilty to Mass Murder Involving Samurai Sword," Honolulu Star Advertiser, July 24, 2015, http://www.staradvertiser.com/2015/07/24/breaking-news/man-pleads-guilty-to-mass-murder-involving-samurai-sword/.

[11] E. McLaughlin, "Tourists Among 22 Killed in Apparent Attack on Bangkok Shrine," CNN, August 17, 2015, http://www.cnn.com/2015/08/17/asia/thailand-bangkok-bomb/.

[12] E. Friedman, "Va. Tech Shooter Seung-Hui Cho's Mental Health Records Released," ABC News, August 19, 2009, http://abcnews.go.com/US/seung-hui-chos-mental-health-records-released/story?id=8278195.

CHAPTER FIVE

SECURITY AND SURVIVAL MINDSETS

KEY LEARNING POINTS:

1. Persistently maintaining a *security mindset* should be part of your everyday life. Those in the military and law enforcement refer to this state as *situational awareness.*

2. If you *prepare your mind in advance*, your chances of survival increase.

3. When faced with a life or death situation, you will react in one of three ways: fight, flight, or freeze. "Freeze" will get you killed.

4. *Proactive reactionism* is the ability to react appropriately to something you've never experienced because you've already planned your response. It requires forethought in the form of anticipation and planning and mental rehearsal until *your plan becomes second nature.*

5. Visualization is the ability to envision by means of imagination an event before it unfolds. It allows you to mentally walk yourself through a successful response if ever

you encounter an active killer. This enables you to be "proactively reactionary".

W hile there are many definitions that explain exactly what mindset is, the one that best relates to the mindset needed to survive an active shooter is "a fixed mental attitude or disposition that predetermines a person's responses to, and interpretations of, situations" (Dictionary.com). What does this mean in real-life terms, and perhaps more importantly, why does it matter so much in this scenario?

Put simply, it is your *mindset* (the way you think) that will predetermine how you'll react in each situation. Thus, if you want to react effectively if you ever find yourself face-to-face with an active shooter, creating this type of life-saving reaction begins with your thoughts.

For example, if you believe that the only way to effectively settle a disagreement with your spouse is to give in and say that you're wrong—even when you don't believe you are—then that is exactly what you'll do. Conversely, if you feel that marital arguments can only be settled when you stand your ground and never give in, then that's what you'll do instead. Both are examples of predetermined reactions.

Security Mindset

Having a security mindset should be part of your everyday life. Whether you're going out in public to go grocery shopping for your family or to present a new or innovative business idea to a room full of conference attendees, you should be thinking about how secure the area is, as well as how you'd respond if someone breached that security. In the military and law enforcement, this is referred to as *situational awareness*.

This is extremely important because active shooters like crowded places with lots of people. (Remember that their goal is to kill as many people as quickly as they possibly can.) For them, it's like shooting fish in a barrel. They have the advantage and better odds for their desired outcome.

A notable example of this is the active shootings that occur at places of worship. In fact, a very busy time for my security company is during the high holy days for the Jewish community because synagogues become major targets, so they need extra protection from individuals who are intent on doing them harm.

Survival Mindset

In an active shooter scenario, how you feel about survival plays a critical role in whether that's what you'll do. In other words, it isn't necessarily that one type of response is better than another, but the action you choose in that situation is based on your interpretation of what's happening and what you believe is the right thing to do. Your actions ultimately mirror your beliefs.

This underscores the importance of having a survival mindset in active assailant scenarios. When you have your own safety and security in mind, as well as the safety and security of those around you, you are telling your mind how to respond in that type of situation. You are telling it that your survival comes first, so your mind and body had better act accordingly.

Creating this mindset first involves becoming aware of what is happening in your immediate surroundings, so your mind recognizes the fact that it needs to formulate an appropriate reaction—a reaction that could potentially save your life, as well as the lives of your family, friends, coworkers, or anyone else in your immediate vicinity.

Having this alert mindset makes you more prepared. It helps you plan for how you'll respond to an incident, should it occur, because it makes you think about the incident before it happens. This keeps you from freezing and doing nothing in a violent encounter, which is the one response that will likely get you killed.

Fight, Flight, or Freeze

When you're faced with a life-or-death situation, your body will have one of three possible reactions. It will either want to fight, flee, or freeze. Fight is when you decide to take on the attacker one-on-one, determined to overpower him or her, so that if anyone survives the event, it is going to be you.

The second option is flight; this is when you escape the dangerous situation. For example, if you're leaving the mall and approach your car only to find someone hiding nearby and ready to attack, you run away before giving the attacker the chance. You evade the situation so your attacker can't execute his or her plan.

The third possible response is the most dangerous, and that is to freeze. This is when you are completely paralyzed and unable to move, which also means that you can't fight off the attacker, and you're unable to flee. This makes you a sitting duck for the person intent on doing you harm, which is the worst possible place to find yourself in. Unfortunately we have found this is an all too common response to this type of event because the victims simply were not mentally prepared to react.

A notable example of this occurred during the incident mentioned earlier, when an armed man walked into a school board meeting to take revenge for the fact that his wife had been fired. In the video of this event I show in my in-person training, you see that once the first shot is fired by the intended assailant, only one board member immediately dives under the board room desk to use cover and concealment. Most of the people being shot at simply freeze, even after several minutes of hearing from the armed man himself that he is going to kill them, in shock at what is occurring with no predetermined reaction to save themselves.

An example is seen in the March 2019 livestreamed video by Brenton Harrison when he entered one of two mosques in Christchurch, New Zealand. After shooting individuals standing in the doorway and hall, he walked into the great room and found dozens of people huddled together, face down, in two corners of the room, where he proceeded to fire into the mass of bodies. He then walked over to both groups of people and shot them again individually to ensure they suffered fatal wounds, ultimately killing 51 and injuring 49.

Though these people didn't freeze completely where they stood, they ran to a corner and laid down, motionless, hoping the shooter would pass them by. They did nothing to increase their chances of survival. And though I'm very sympathetic to these people and the people that will miss them, the hard, cold reality is that if they had done *anything* other than what they did, they would have had a much greater probability of survival.

I go further in depth in Chapter 9 about how effectively a small group of people can overcome a shooter, and even if one or two are shot, they can successfully take the killer down. There were more than two dozen people in this room who could have charged the shooter, or even surprised him when he entered the room, mitigating the shooter's ability to fire his weapon and saving multiple lives. Because these people were never taught how to properly react to an active shooter, they simply didn't understand that engaging the shooter may have resulted in some injury or even death, but doing nothing resulted in the death of almost everyone there.

So how do you get the type of mindset that enables you to respond appropriately in an active shooter scenario, so you don't freeze, increasing your chances of survival? You begin to think with your *survival* in mind.

The Pollyanna Effect

The *Pollyanna Principle* is the tendency for people to remember pleasant experiences more accurately than experiences which are unpleasant. The *Pollyanna Effect* occurs when one's subconscious bias toward the positive causes them to view the world around them in an overwhelmingly positive fashion. Some label this behavior as living in a state of *denial.*

Sadly, there are many Pollyannas in this world. These are the people who have difficulty seeing the dark side of humanity because they're always seeking the positives in life; they are the *sheep*, who find it difficult to see or predict when someone is intent on committing harm.

Generally, this isn't a bad thing because it means that you have empathy, that you're able to see beyond a person's bad behavior when that behavior isn't necessarily their intent. However, if this is you, you may also struggle with creating a security mindset.

As a Pollyanna, you don't want to see the evil in this world. But the problem with this mindset is that because there *is* evil in this world, you are left completely unprepared and unable to recognize when you find yourself looking at someone who doesn't fit in or looks threatening. You can't easily see the potential problem because you only want to see the good.

Ultimately, this mindset will work against you in the preparedness for or response to an active assailant. Not that I'm saying you should completely change the way you think, because I'm not. I'm saying that this is how some people think, and it has gotten them injured or killed as a result, so adding a security mindset to your precognitive ideology can keep you alive. That's why it helps to be suspicious when appropriate and to listen to your gut.

Listen to Your Gut

In his book *The Gift of Fear: Survival Signals That Protect Us from Violence*, author Gavin de Becker suggests every individual should learn to trust the inherent "*gift*" of their gut instinct and how this physical response already exists in everyone, making it possible to avoid potential trauma and harm by learning to recognize various warning signs and precursors to violence.

I liken fear to your body's other natural early warning systems, like hunger, thirst, and fatigue. When you're hungry, you know that your body needs fuel. When you're thirsty, there's no denying that if you don't get water within the necessary amount of time, you could perish. And when your body runs out of the necessary energy resources it needs to go on, it must rest and recharge.

Basically, your stomach acts as your second brain. It tells you when it may be necessary to become more alert and hyperaware if you want to survive. While you never allow yourself to become consumed by this gut reaction, you do need to listen to it. You need to pay attention and heed its warning when it tells you that something just doesn't feel right.

When you feel fear, like when you're in a dark alley or an unfamiliar environment at night with limited visibility and suddenly feel the hair stand up on the back of your neck, yet no one's in sight, your body and your mind are telling you to be on high alert. Something may be amiss, even if you can't quite put your finger on what.

My dad was a master at this. As a former law enforcement officer and the founder of our company, he watched people and, more often than not, they were not a potential threat. But he was always observant and became hyperaware when people didn't fit in, which is when his level of alertness was piqued. As a result, whenever someone whose appearance or behavior stood out as unusual you could tell he was processing not only what potential threat that person could be, if any, but how to respond to the threat to protect himself and those around him. He was always situationally aware. An often used comment by my father's many friends and associates after his passing was, "I always felt safe around your dad."

Developing Situational Awareness

An extreme example of situational awareness is the character Jason Bourne in the Bourne series. In one scene of the movie *The Bourne Identity*, Bourne and his female companion are sitting in a restaurant when he explains to her how he sees everything. He begins talking about the first thing he noticed when he came into the restaurant. He shares how he was "catching sidelines" and "looking for the exit."

Bourne goes on to reveal that he could tell her the license plate numbers of all six cars in the parking lot and that he knows the best place to look for a gun is the cab of the gray truck outside. He knows that "the waitress is left-handed, and the guy at the counter weighs 215 pounds and knows how to handle himself"; he knows every other detail he's picked up on that could potentially help him if confronted by a threat. He even says he knows his own personal physical limits, stating that "at this altitude, I can run flat out for half a mile before my hands start shaking."

You want to train your mind to react to situations with this type of detail and clarity so you're always prepared, should they occur. Okay, perhaps not as prepared as Jason Bourne, but you get the point. This is something I call being *proactively reactionary*.

Proactive Reactionism

Proactive reactionism is a term I created, so you won't find it in any dictionary. What it involves is the idea that you can train yourself to react appropriately to something you've never experienced if you prepare your mind in advance.

This type of proactive physical and mental reaction works because you:

1. Imagine a scenario before it occurs.

2. Have a plan for that scenario.

3. Make the plan become second nature.

How does this type of training translate into a positive response to an active shooter situation? In times of stress, people default to their level of training. For instance, in one study, people were interviewed after performing the Heimlich maneuver or CPR to save someone's life. When asked about the event, they responded that they had training years ago and, even surprising themselves, that training and knowledge just came back to them in that instant when someone's life was in jeopardy. Their minds defaulted to the training that they had taken years ago and they immediately began the steps necessary when the time came, moving that knowledge from the back of their minds (subconscious) to the front (conscious), ultimately making it possible to save the person's life.

It's kind of the same principle as riding a bike. You may go 10, 20, or 30 years without placing your butt on a bicycle seat, but once you do, you might be a little rusty, but you pick right up where you left off. The same is true regarding training in active shooter scenarios. Once you internalize and tell your body how to respond, that's likely what it'll do if you're ever confronted with someone who is intent on doing you harm.

That, of course, does not mean you should simply learn this or any other type of life-saving knowledge and take for granted that when you need it, it will be there. Once practiced enough it will be in your conscious, not subconscious, so the time it will take to recall it will be even less, and when your life is in peril, the less time it takes to act, the better.

Some people are taught these types of responses from childhood. For instance, as I have stated, I had a father who was in law enforcement, so I witnessed his behavior and often emulated it naturally even prior to many years of training in later life. But if you weren't raised that way or didn't have that example when you were growing up, let me assure you that it's never too late to learn. Survival can easily become your first reaction, your fixed mindset. But the understanding of exactly how to survive has changed over time, which is why I created the A.L.I.V.E. *Active Shooter Survival Plan.*

The reason the A.L.I.V.E. program is different and more effective than other active shooter survival programs is that I teach not just method but also mindset as equal parts. You can have the greatest knowledge of procedure, technique, and method to carry out a plan, but if you don't have the mindset to properly execute the method, it will never be as effective. And in the situation of surviving an active shooter, mindset is just as important to your survival as method.

Proactive Reactionism and Visualization: Creating a Plan Before You Need It

Visualization exercises help a lot in this type of situation as they allow you to create a mental plan. They walk you through many different scenarios and force you to think about what could possibly happen. They also set the stage for you to plan your response, so if you're ever faced with someone intent on taking your life, you'll already know what to do.

Another benefit of visualization is that while you can't possibly physically train for every potential violent encounter in your life, you can train mentally very easily because all you need is your imagination and a little bit of free time. This is a technique that many law enforcement and other public safety responders are taught early in their careers as a way of increasing their safety when responding to what are sometimes harrowing situations.

This simple visualization works by imagining a scenario in which you're faced with an active killer. As you envision this event unfolding before you, mentally walk yourself through a successful response.

When performing your visualization, run through the scenario multiple times until it feels like you have your response ingrained in your mind. Then, once you're comfortable with your response, change the scenario. This forces you to consider other alternatives and modify your plan accordingly. For instance, imagine the killer entering through a different door, carrying a different weapon, or even looking physically different. The more possible plans you have in place, the more readily and the better you will respond.

During this process, imagine all the same details as you would during the experience. Hear the sounds, smell the smells, see in your mind's eye everything you would naturally and in real life. Ideally, you want to use as many of your senses as you can while visualizing. This makes the situation as realistic to your mind as possible, and the more your brain feels like you're in an actual encounter, the better equipped it will be to carry out your plan when needed.

For example, let's say you imagine an active killer entering your workplace. If this happens, what noises are you likely to hear just prior to and during the event? Machines humming, coworkers talking, phones ringing? When the shooting starts, imagine people running, screaming, the sound of gunshots. What stands between you and the killer? Plexiglas windows? Nothing? What limits will you have to your sight that could put you in harm's way? Is your view blocked by a cabinet or wall? Are you in a cubicle or your own office? Are there locks on your doors you can use? What do you have at your disposal to use as a weapon if necessary? Your goal is to try to imagine the scenario as realistically as you can.

Before proceeding, please take a few moments to go through the visualization process now, preferably using a few different scenarios. Take notice of your emotional state when you've finished. Are you scared, anxious, angry? Do you feel helpless, or determined to survive using any and all means necessary?

Now that you've imagined what you would do before learning the essential steps of survival using A.L.I.V.E., keep in mind what you just imagined in your own visualization while you learn them. In other words, as you learn each step of A.L.I.V.E., think about how you would apply that information to your own personal scenarios.

Okay, now that you understand that it CAN happen to you, anytime and anywhere, why those first 10 precious minutes matter so much to your survival, why the active killer does what they do, and where your mindset should be before such an event and how you must think once an active shooter event begins, let's delve into the essential, lifesaving five-step plan you can use to dramatically increase your chances of surviving such a horrible event.

The A.L.I.V.E. Active Shooter Survival Plan

A ASSESS

L LEAVE

I IMPEDE

V VIOLENCE

E EXPOSE

®

CHAPTER SIX

ASSESS

KEY LEARNING POINTS:

1. If under attack, *examine what is happening and your surroundings before you move.* ASSESS your situation, don't just move blindly and hope for the best.
2. Consider which of the next steps of A.L.I.V.E. is the best choice to help you survive. Can you LEAVE, should you try to IMPEDE the killer, or is you only choice to engage the assailant with extreme VIOLENCE?
3. Initiating contact with law enforcement immediately is absolutely essential to start the clock ticking toward the conclusion of the event.

When faced with an active killer situation, the first thing you want to do is ASSESS the situation: stop, take a deep breath, and think about what may be happening around you. This helps keep you from panicking, delivers a full shot of oxygen to your brain to aid in remaining calm (your adrenaline will start pumping and your heart pounding, so you'll need all the oxygen you can get to feed your body and brain), and allows you to respond in a way that will maximize your safety while putting your response plan into action rationally rather than emotionally.

The worst possible time to create a plan is when you're in the middle of a crisis. That would be like not thinking about how you'd escape your second-floor bedroom in the event of a fire yet waking up one night to flames in the only stairwell in your house. Your failure to plan could easily mean you don't make it out alive. At a minimum, it will raise your stress level and delay your response as you try to quickly think about your options while the flames grow closer and closer.

This is also why training with active killer scenarios is important, or at the very least practicing your visualization exercise. The more you know how you want to respond before you need to, the more you're able to respond calmly and rationally, and the better your response will be. Furthermore, the better your response is, the greater your likelihood of survival.

Decide Your Plan

If you suddenly realize that you're in an active killer scenario, it is during the assessment phase that you want to think about which plan to put into action. Thus, you'll need to consider your plan as it relates to the incident. Think about your options as they relate to your plan.

For instance, will you be able to safely and effectively LEAVE the area, or are you going to have to stay and engage the assailant? If you must attack, what objects are in your vicinity that you could use as weapons? Is anyone there who could help you overpower and take down the attacker or attackers?

All in all, you want to think about your plan and ASSESS your situation before you act. Your only goal at this point is to determine which of your next actions are most appropriate. Think about what is happening around you and about your options in relation to the events.

In the second part, live scenario and simulation portion of the A.L.I.V.E. training, we simulate an active shooter in whatever setting I'm giving the training, preferably right where the audience works or spends most of their day. When I give the command, everyone decides, through their assessment of the situation, whether they will LEAVE, can only IMPEDE the killer, or if they must commit to VIOLENCE against them. They then take the appropriate action and follow through until the exercise is completed, at which time they EXPOSE their position, carefully.

This exercise is conducted several times, in various areas of the building when possible, to create different plans for each scenario. Then those plans can be practiced, or drilled, so when reacting to each specific scenario, if an active shooter event ever does occur, the appropriate reaction will be second nature.

Don't Just "Run"

While it may be tempting or second nature to just take off running, that may be the last thing you want to do. What you think might be the right direction to go—a way out—may take you into the center of the incident instead.

The better approach, the safer approach, is to be methodical. If you do move, move briskly, but when you come to a corner or any other area that impairs your line of sight, look around it first to see what's on the other side, unless of course the shooter is behind you. Don't just move blindly and hope for the best.

Even though you may be hearing sounds coming from one direction, that doesn't necessarily tell you which way safety lies. Halls tend to echo, and the acoustics can be deceiving, so you might not be able to tell the killer's location based on the noises you're hearing.

Pause and ASSESS for a split second to gather your thoughts and take control of your conscious next steps. Give your brain that brief moment it needs to let whatever is happening sink in so you can consider your full situation and surroundings, logically rather than emotionally, before deciding what to do next.

Isn't Pausing Dangerous?

During one of my trainings, in front of a very large audience, I once had a student challenge the idea of pausing and assessing one's surroundings before acting. He argued, "But if you wait, the guy might come there and kill you." Maybe you've even had this very same thought yourself. If so, let's clear this up right now. I assure you that when your adrenaline hits, which it will during an event like this, you will be able to think several minutes' worth of thoughts in just seconds. If you've ever been in a life-or-death situation, then you already know this is true.

When threatened, your mind will go faster than you've ever thought possible. Consider the old saying, "my life flashed before my eyes" and you'll understand this a little better. One can relive a lifetime of memories in the blink of an eye in this type of situation. And these few short seconds could be the difference between acting rashly with emotion and methodically with reason.

So taking a quick moment to fully ASSESS the situation around you isn't going to slow you down because it's going to be happening at faster-than-normal speeds. Have you ever needed to stop quickly while driving? If so, it is likely that over time you learned by means of experience and conscious decision-making to unconsciously ASSESS the *danger*, consider your *options*, and instantly react, and in doing so possibly saved your life or the lives of others. Confronting an active killer is no different. You must practice allowing your mind to process. If you don't, you'll likely react irrationally and panic, or freeze.

Prepare to Kill or Be Killed

When you're assessing the situation, this is also the time to start ramping yourself up mentally, preparing your mind to kill or be killed. You need to be ready to take some type of action, no matter what that action is, to save your own life and possibly the lives of those around you.

This is a difficult concept for some people, but it's one that is necessary if you want to survive. Remember, the active killer's goal is to take out as many people as quickly as possible. He or she doesn't care that you have a family, a job, or so many wonderful things to live for. All he cares about is ending your life before moving on to the next victim, and the next.

That's why your assessment of the situation, of your options as they relate to your specific incident, should include formulating the attitude that if anyone is going home today, it's going to be you. You need to decide at the very beginning of the event that you'll do whatever is necessary to protect your life.

Now that you've determined what your best option for survival is, you MUST call 911 immediately! I explain in more detail as to why it is absolutely imperative to get law enforcement on scene as soon as possible in future chapters, but understand right now, the sooner emergency response arrives, the sooner the assailant will divert his attention away from you, be immobilized by law enforcement, or take his own life. The result is the same—he isn't focused on killing you any longer.

Once you've assessed the situation and reaffirmed in your mind that you'll take as much action as is necessary to survive the incident, it's time to move on to the next step. If during your assessment you've concluded that escape is an option, it is now time to LEAVE.

CHAPTER SEVEN

LEAVE

KEY LEARNING POINTS:

1. If you can LEAVE, *put as much distance and matter between you and the threat as you can.*
2. If running directly away from a shooter, veer right or left when possible. A target moving from one side to the other is harder to hit than a straight line away.
3. Stay low and run where obstacles block the killer's line of sight of you.
4. When notifying others that they need to evacuate, you must be *commanding in your tone and presence.*
5. Leave behind everything but your cell phone, weapon, and protective garment if you have them.

I t's often said that the best fight is the one that's avoided, and this rings especially true in active killer incidents. Because the attacker's primary goal is to kill as many people as possible as quickly as possible, if you can get away and escape to a safe area, that's by far the best thing you can do.

It wasn't long ago that a *lockdown* was the first response to a report of criminal activity or a sighting of a predator or active shooter around schools. But we've learned we will likely not know about active killers until after they have already entered the building or after the killing begins. As such, locking down may be the wrong response when leaving is still possible. At least until all schools, medical facilities and office buildings have either been retrofitted or new construction has implemented appropriate safe room mechanisms to eliminate the possibility of an intruder gaining access to occupied rooms. And mark my words, you will see this happen in the next few years.

Get Away from the Threat—Fast!

Get as far away from the threat as quickly as you possibly can while you are calling 911. Remember, the sooner you get law enforcement en route to your location, the sooner the shooter may kill themselves or their attention will be diverted away from potential victims and onto the police. This means that once you've assessed the situation, decided which plan to put into action, and determined your most viable and accessible escape route, you want to run as fast as you can, as far away as you can.

Even if you're not in the best physical shape possible, push your legs to move you as fast as they humanly can. The adrenaline released by your system will help, enabling you to go quicker than you would under normal, non-stressful circumstances.

Don't stop running until you're someplace where the killer can't harm you, or if you are being shot at, get something between you and the killer to provide cover while continuing to create distance. Depending on your location and the incident, this may involve heading to a neighboring business or building, running through a parking lot full of vehicles, or finding some other place that is beyond the killer's reach.

A moving target is difficult to hit with a firearm, but you can make it even more difficult in the way that you move. If a shooter is behind you in a hallway, zigzag from one side to the other if possible. A target moving away from a gunman is easier to hit if that target is only moving away in a straight line. In this instance, the target is only getting smaller, but the site picture remains the same. The shooter only has to deal with vertical movement rather than also keeping their site steady from left to right. Don't be an easy target.

If you are in a larger indoor or outdoor space, move in a direction that you can place objects between you. In a parking lot, concert hall, or open area, try to stay low while still moving as rapidly as possible, using as much cover as you can. That means placing any available objects between you and the shooter to make it difficult for them to see you, or to stop or deflect bullets as they travel toward you.

Obviously, the distance you must go to be considered "safe" will be determined by the type of weapon the active killer is using. However, remember that in most cases, active killers bring several different weapons to the attack. So don't just assume that he or she only has one. Run as if there are several weapons, and don't stop running until you're as far away as you can safely go.

Notify Those Around You

In addition to getting yourself out of the area, you also want to notify everyone in your immediate vicinity of control about what you believe is happening. Share with them that it's possible (unless you know for sure) an active killer is near you, so you need to go, and you need to go now!

If they've had this training too (which is highly possible if they're coworkers that attended one of my classes hosted by your organization), they'll know exactly what to do. That's why I always recommend everyone in an organization have an opportunity to attend the training. The more you can work as a group, the more effective your response will be.

If they haven't had this training, be ready to tell them exactly what they must do. This is important because without proper training, they may want to do something that could inevitably put them, and you, in greater danger. You can help prevent that by giving some direction.

When notifying others to LEAVE, you must be *commanding in your tone and presence.* That means you need to be assertive, to take control. There's usually one person in every group who will automatically step into this role (sheepdogs), but if your group doesn't have one, then that person needs to be you.

Notify those around you with the appropriate force and volume: "Get out now!" or "Run as far and as fast as you can!" Be firm and direct. Sound like you mean business, using the same tone of voice you would if you saw a young child reaching for a hot stove. Then, as a group, LEAVE the area of danger and don't stop running until you are too far away to be harmed.

When You're Responsible for Others

If you're responsible for others, you want to usher them with commanding urgency as well. This could occur if you're a daycare provider or a teacher at a school. As a nurse on a hospital ward, you'd be responsible for your patients, and as a hotel manager, you're responsible for your guests. And of course, if you are a security professional, providing a safe and secure environment is a primary function of your presence, so be ready to take command of the area and those around you and get people to safety or prepare for the next steps of the A.L.I.V.E. Plan.

If you're an employer or someone who is in a supervisory role, then you're responsible for your staff. Take charge and use authority when telling them to LEAVE. If you must, direct them where to go. If the group requires it, such as may occur if you're responsible for a second-grade class or individuals with disabilities, then you may also need to lead the way.

Think about these things when visualizing your plan. The more you know what to do beforehand, the easier it will be for you to keep your calm while establishing control.

Where is the best place to direct them to go, or to go yourself if you're on your own? Your preplanning and preparation should assist you making these important and often spontaneous decisions.

Where to Go?

If the incident is occurring inside a building and you can exit that building, run as far away as possible, trying to keep objects between you and the shooter for cover. Again, the more distance you can put between you and the killer, the safer you will be.

If you can't get out, or if it's closer than getting out, run to a secure location, like a safe room if one is available. Ideally, this is a room where you can lock and barricade the door. It's also a room with either a small window or no window at all, or a window that can be blocked off, so the killer can't see inside or get through.

The best safe rooms are also rooms that can stop or dramatically slow down flying bullets. For instance, if there's a room available that has block walls and one that has just drywall, the room with block walls is your better option because the walls have more stopping power. Only by increasing the distance from the target, and matter the bullet must pass through, can one diminish the penetrating power of the weapon used against them. Generally, if a nail can be driven though your chosen barrier with one or two hits of a carpenter's hammer, a handgun or rifle round can penetrate that same barrier.

Whether you LEAVE the area entirely or go to a safe room, leave your belongings behind. Well, most of them, anyway.

LEAVE (Most of) Your Belongings Behind

If you've ever flown in an airplane, you've probably observed the required FAA preflight safety briefing. And if you've heard it more than once you know that in the event of an emergency requiring evacuation, you must leave all your belongings behind. Doing so leaves you with one task: getting yourself out of the aircraft.

That makes sense, right? Can you imagine how long it would take to evacuate everyone if all the passengers went for their carry-ons first? Or what if you were denied access to one of the rafts because there wasn't any more room, yet it was half full with personal effects and/or carry-ons? The same advice applies here for the same general reasons. Gathering your things will delay your escape, and the last thing you want is a large purse or briefcase weighing you down when you're trying to evade an active killer. But there are exceptions to this rule.

1. If you have a weapon, you want to take that with you if you can get access to it quickly and safely. This way, you'll have it if you are forced to commit VIOLENCE against the active killer; your weapon isn't going to do you any good if you've left it behind.

Some law enforcement representatives might argue that a civilian having a gun in this situation is ill-advised, if for no other reason than officer safety. I understand and appreciate this school of thought. However, as someone who grew up with guns and has trained with and used them on many occasions, I know that if I have a gun, I'm taking it with me! Just be sure to keep your weapon down and behind you unless you need it, and to drop it, raise your hands, and step away from it immediately if you see law enforcement. Remember that the responding officers aren't going to know who the good guys are and who the bad guys are; you don't want them to mistake you for the shooter. And if you do have a weapon, all rules of safety still apply, including not shooting unless you're absolutely sure of the target and what is beyond it.

2. You should have already been calling 911 so should still have your cell phone with you. This enables you to continue to communicate with law enforcement, so you can report back to them what you know, and they can advise you on any information they have, which could potentially keep you from running right into the shooter. Keep in mind that a response that is five seconds faster not only saves the lives of potential victims but also means the killer can be stopped more quickly. Law enforcement will detain the active killer or kill him to stop the threat, or the killer will take his own life.

3. The topic of training small children to respond to an active shooter is a delicate one, and I'm careful to offer my opinion without additional research into child psychology and behavior (perhaps that will be my next book), so I'm a bit hesitant in my next listed exception. If children do happen to have bulletproof backpacks on (a highly promoted survival apparatus on the market that, as of the date of this writing, had not actually been "battle tested" in an active shooter situation) when an active shooter event breaks out, I do not believe they

should drop them before or while attempting to LEAVE the scene. I do, however, promote leaving those backpacks where they are if it means delaying their escape by adding steps to retrieve them when leading them to safety or to a saferoom.

In these scenarios, the result is the same. The threat is over, and your decision to LEAVE the scene enabled you, and maybe others, to survive the attack.

If you're not able to LEAVE, it becomes necessary to do something else—and the next best response is to IMPEDE the active killer.

CHAPTER EIGHT

IMPEDE

KEY LEARNING POINTS:

1. If you are unable to LEAVE, seek shelter and *put barriers between you and the killer to IMPEDE their ability to get to you.*

2. Cover and concealment are not the same thing. *Cover provides physical protection*, concealment simply prevents you from being seen.

3. When employed properly, locking and blocking can provide both cover and concealment.

4. When calling 911 for help, remain on the line but *keep your phone on silent.*

5. Hiding under a desk or table is not hiding if you can be seen from multiple angles.

I mpeding an active killer means that you need to do everything possible to limit his or her opportunity and ability to get to you. Your goal is to be so difficult to reach that it's not worth the killer's limited time to try.

The reason this works to your advantage is that in most instances, assailants will take the path of least resistance. This makes sense because their goal is to take as many lives as they can in as little time as possible. Therefore, they're not going to spend a lot of time trying to get you if you make yourself a hard target, which is precisely why you want to be difficult to find and difficult to get to.

In a situation where you are in an open area and unable to barricade yourself in a room or to find an area that is difficult to access, impeding may not be possible. To make yourself a hard target, you need to find cover, or at least something that's going to conceal you. What's the difference?

Cover Versus Concealment

Concealment basically means that you're hidden from view. For instance, if you stood behind a shower curtain in a bathroom, you'd be concealed, as anyone who walked by the room wouldn't see you there.

Cover, on the other hand, is an object that may not completely hide you from view but would likely stop a bullet from reaching and striking you (which a shower curtain would not do). Good examples of cover include a thick wooden table, a sturdy bookshelf loaded with books, or the engine block of a car.

If you've ever played paintball, it's likely that you already know the difference between concealment and cover. Cover will stop the paintball from striking you, hitting whatever is between you and the shooter. Concealment means that if the shooter can't see you, he either won't know you're there or will have a difficult time getting you in his site picture. Clearly the best scenario is if you can use both to your advantage.

At the first indication of danger or a possible active shooter event in progress, if you cannot LEAVE, look around you and take in your surroundings to find the best place to go, the place that is out of eyesight of the active killer. The safer the area where you hunker down, the better your chances of survival.

If you can't LEAVE you want to find cover, just in case you find yourself in the killer's line of fire. But that's not always possible. Sometimes you are only presented with the option of concealing yourself, which is certainly better than nothing at all.

When I was a kid growing up in Northern Colorado, my friends and I would battle each other using BB guns. (I know, brilliant, right?) We knew we had to keep ourselves away from our "enemies", so knowing where they were at all times was essential to avoiding being shot.

In a situation where an active shooter is in an open location with multiple targets, he will typically aim at the closest and most easily engaged targets, or into a crowd for the greatest likelihood of hitting people. It's your objective to remain hidden, if the shooter doesn't already know where you are, or get behind cover, making it more difficult to hit you. However, the shooter will likely be walking around looking for new targets, so you still need to know where the shooter is and adjust your position or cover to avoid becoming a victim.

A childhood BB gun fight is a very simplified example, but the principles of evasion are the same. You are still in a situation where someone's intent is to hit you with a deadly projectile, so your objective is to stay out of view and/or make it difficult to hit you. This means that you'll need to be aware of the shooter's position as much as possible.

And if you do find your way to a room, there are many things you can do once there to IMPEDE the killer and make yourself a more difficult target. One option is to lock and block.

Lock and Block

Lock and block refers to the process you want to follow when securing the door, so the killer cannot get through it and gain access to the room you are in.

The first part of this is simply a reminder to lock the door if you can. Sometimes this alone is enough to stop a killer from entering because either he or she thinks the room is empty or you've made it harder to get at you, so the killer moves on to other, easier targets. Sadly, at many organization where I present this survival plan, most do not even have locks on their conference or copy room doors, which is unfortunate because this is a very simple fix that could potentially save lives.

The second part of the lock-and-block process involves blocking the door so the killer cannot easily gain entry. Even if the door does lock, you should still take this additional step to better protect yourself and anyone else in the room. In the off chance the active shooter attempts to shoot the lock and hinges on the door to gain entry, which to date has not been known to have occurred, if there are cases of paper, wooden desks, file cabinets, or other heavy, solid objects barricading the door, it will not be worth their time to attempt entry while delaying or restricting their objective.

If the door has a window in it, block that off as well. Lots of door windows have shades you can pull to disrupt the view, which is what I recommend when consulting with business owners and managers who would like to improve the safety of their businesses.

If your door doesn't have a shade or a blind, then just find something to cover it. Pieces of paper taped up, a curtain pulled from an outside window, or even your shirt or jacket will do the trick.

Using lock and block slows the shooter down, so he or she will likely pass that door to pursue easier targets of opportunity. It also keeps the shooter from seeing who is inside and shooting into the room if he cannot see in.

An example of why this is important is when Nicolas Cruz returned to Marjory Stoneman Douglas High School in Parkland, Florida, the high school he previously attended, and opened fire on students, he never actually entered either of the two classrooms he shot into. Instead, he shot through the small windows in the doors, killing students inside. If the doors were locked and he couldn't have seen his targets, he would likely have passed by looking for easy targets.

To this end, I would also recommend that anyone inside a room go to what is termed a "hard corner". This is the area inside the room that cannot be seen if the killer is looking through a window. In the diagram of a classroom below you will see the lower left corner, shaded in light blue, is beyond sight of the shooter, seen standing at the door. The area in red is the part of the classroom the shooter can see. This of course applies in any room, office, or other facility compartment.

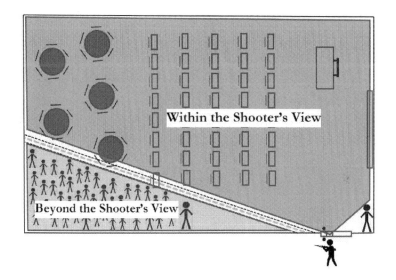

Besides being out of sight, remaining quiet is also key. You must place your cell phone on silent so incoming texts and calls don't attract the killer's attention. If the news is already broadcasting the event, or others are aware of what is transpiring, you will likely begin getting texts and calls from friends and loved ones to find out if you are safe. The last thing you want is yours or anyone else's cell phone going off just as a shooter has decided to bypass your location because he or she believes no one is present.

Remember: your primary goal if you're unable to LEAVE the area is to be difficult to find and difficult to get to, so secure your location as best you can.

Securing the Door

There are a couple of ways to better secure the door to a room, regardless of whether it locks or not. For instance, if it opens in, and you don't have some type of intruder-defense device (which I recommend all businesses acquire and conduct drills with), you can use a simple door wedge to help make it more difficult to open. When using a door wedge (the type used to stop an opened door from closing), it must have the appropriate underside to work with the flooring in your facility. A hard wedge on a tile floor would not be as effective as a rubber wedge on carpet, but it can still work. To reinforce its effectiveness, you could place your foot, or some other heavy item like a file cabinet, behind the wedge but keep your body very low or to the side of the door in the unlikely event the shooter tries shooting through the door.

Another way is to block the door with everything possible, putting the heaviest items against it first. If you block the door physically with your body, again, stay low and close to the floor or off to the side to avoid shots if the killer has a gun and decides to fire in your direction.

If the door opens out (like doors that have a scissor arm at the top), and you don't have a predesigned intruder-defense device, you can always use a belt to keep the scissors together, making it more difficult to open. If you don't have a belt, use an extension or computer monitor cord, or anything else you can find to constrict the door closer.

You can also secure the handle on an outward-opening door so it can't easily be pulled open. This can be accomplished with a belt or any other item that you can latch onto and either hold or secure to something else in the room. Again, even if the door does open out, you still want to block it with everything possible, placing the heaviest items closest to the door.

Notify

If possible, you should have already notified emergency services. But if you couldn't do that and must hide and remain quiet, many law enforcement agencies now have the capability to receive notifications of an emergency through text message using text-to-911, so you can advise dispatch of the situation and communicate with them as the scene unfolds. They will be able to relay information to you from their officers, so you may be able to escape if the shooter has moved to the other side of the building.

There are also public announcement applications for smartphones, frequently used on college campuses now, that will not only notify you of the presence of an active killer but also advise you as the situation progresses. Some use the GPS functionality of our phone to identify you so emergency services using that technology knows who and where you are. You will see more and more of these technological advances to aid in active shooter survival used in educational and health-care facilities, and in businesses.

There may even be times when someone is able to advise you using an audible public announcement system to notify you where the shooter is and the status of the event. Many businesses use VOIP (Voice Over IP) phone systems, and one of the functionalities is mass notification and intercom. Learn how to use this feature if you work in a building that has this technology.

Qualities of a Practical but Adequate Safe Room

Having access to a safe room would be a tremendous advantage and best-case scenario in surviving an active killer event. For a room to be considered sufficiently safe during an active killer incident but still practical enough to not be excessive in an office environment, it should have the following qualities: the most basic safe room is simply a closet, copy room, or internal conference room with an exterior-grade, solid-core door that has a dead bolt and longer hinge screws and strike-plate screws to resist battering. Sometimes the ceiling is reinforced or gated to prevent easy access from an attic, overhead crawl space, or drop ceiling.

More expensive safe rooms have walls and a door reinforced with sheets of steel, Kevlar, or bullet-resistant fiberglass. The hinges and strike plate are often reinforced with long screws. Some safe rooms may also have externally routed ventilation systems and a separate telephone connection. They might also connect to an escape shaft. Rooms like this are often expensive and therefore not common in a corporate environment.

Any room intended to be utilized as a safe room in the case of a violent attack should have a video intercom, like those made by BEC Integrated Solutions or Docooler for less than $200, so people inside the room can see and hear who is outside. This way, innocent people can be seen and verified when trying to enter the room, and the attacker's actions and whereabouts can be monitored if they nearby.

Being aware of these types of qualities can help you pick the safest room possible, especially if the incident occurs someplace you're familiar with, like at work. This enables you to preselect the rooms you'd go to, if possible, during an active killer incident.

Secondarily, if you own a business or are somehow responsible for employee safety, you can build a safe room into your office plans. If your building or space is already established, you can still modify certain areas to make them safer for your staff and anyone else who may be visiting your facility.

What Hide Does NOT Mean

During the Columbine incident, several of the students got under skinny-legged tables in the library to hide. The problem with this type of response is that the two shooters could easily see their victims. They essentially became easy targets because not only were they not behind cover, they weren't even really concealed. Unfortunately, if those kids had kept running like others did, they would have almost certainly escaped and lived. Instead, at least four children lost their lives because they followed their programming to get under a desk or table in an emergency.

For this reason, it has become imperative to teach students the difference between hiding under their desks or tables and hiding in a place that provides effective cover and concealment, depending on the event. In the case of a violent attack, this way of hiding simply makes them sitting ducks. Old reaction methods are not effective in modern-day active killer scenarios. Instead, innovative approaches need to be created, and one of them is to not just hide, but to hide in a spot that gives you the best chance of survival.

Regardless of how well you hide, though, sometimes it's just not enough. Sometimes you're faced with no other option but to use VIOLENCE and attack.

CHAPTER NINE

VIOLENCE

KEY LEARNING POINTS:

1. An active killer cannot be reasoned with or dissuaded. If he has decided to kill, the only way to stop him it to *disarm or even kill him first.*
2. The killer wants to end your life. *That power and control they gain from this is all they desire.* They want you and those around you dead.
3. Find a weapon, any weapon. Arm yourself with anything you can find in your immediate vicinity to use against the attacker when able.
4. When *swarming*, your first goal should be to *control the weapon, then control the killer.*

I never liked the word "fight" to describe acting against an active killer because to me, a fight typically denotes a battle between two entities with equal resources and chances to prevail. This isn't a duel, gun fight at high noon, or two boxers stepping into the ring. This is a situation where one (most likely) person has a gun and the people he is trying to kill probably do not.

So the "V" in A.L.I.V.E. is for VIOLENCE. Although violence is typically thought of as a negative word by some, in this case, it may very well be the deciding factor in your survival if you're ever in a confrontation with an active killer. Just like the color red evokes a stimulating effect on the brain, the word violence can evoke feelings of anger and hostility. Those are the feelings I want you to have toward your would-be killer so that if you have no other option than to commit VIOLENCE against them, you do so with extreme prejudice.

In this reference, VIOLENCE is just another word for attack, which is what you will need to do if you're unable to LEAVE the area or IMPEDE the killer, and he is close enough to harm you. This may not be easy for you, but you must be of the mindset that it is either you or the killer who is going to die. You must attack the killer with the "intent" to kill because there is no negotiating with an active killer.

Be Prepared to Kill

You cannot hesitate or hold back. Do not try to just maim or injure the killer, wounding them just enough to lessen the threat. The odds are that you will fail and likely make yourself an available target that the killer can turn all his attention, and intention, to bringing you harm. And do not try to talk him or her out of killing you. Active killers are not there to vent or negotiate. They are there to kill as many people as possible in as short a time as possible—end of story!

I know that it sounds terrible to tell you to attack someone with the intent of ending that person's life, but that person wants to kill you. Active killers don't care that you just had a new baby or grandbaby, that you're a good person who always gives back to the community, or that you are a mere four days from retiring and enjoying life. They don't care!

If you are feeling a little disturbed or uneasy that I just told you to kill someone, understand that what I'm referring to is a state of mind. If the killer has been subdued, separated from his weapon, and is no longer a threat, I'm not telling you to end their life at that point. I'm telling you that in order to take action with optimal effectiveness you need to have an extreme mindset. You must match force and intent with equal, but preferably greater, force and intent. They are resolved to kill you. You must have a greater resolve to overcome and succeed in your intention to survive.

The killer wants to end your life. That's it. The sense of power and control they feel in their mind is all they desire. They want you dead and everyone else in the area dead as well.

That's why you need to be 100% committed to the process of taking them out. Not 80% or 90%, because whatever percentage you don't give is now on their side. Rest assured, they will use what you give them to their advantage, so don't give them anything.

Now, if you don't think you could kill someone (I get about one person in every four classes who feels this way), then change the way you look at it. Think about your family. Think about your loved ones. Could you take a life if it meant that you could go home to them? Or if they're with you, could you take a life to make sure they survive?

I often conduct an exercise I call, *Can I take another human life?* with those who say they cannot when I ask during my trainings. I ask the participant's name—we'll call her Mary (they are not always women, but for this demonstration I'll use a female)—and then I ask Mary to mentally picture the person who means the most to her in life. It's usually a child, spouse, partner, parent, brother, or sister. I ask the name of that person, and then I ask for a volunteer from the audience to come up and stand next to me.

At that point, I tell Mary to pretend that volunteer is the person she said meant the most to her. (Let's say it's her son, Jimmy.) I tell Mary to look at the volunteer and picture Jimmy's face. Then I tell Mary to make her hand look like a gun and point it at me. I then make my hand into a gun and point it at Jimmy's head. I tell Mary, "I'm going to count to three, and when I reach three, I'm going to pull the trigger and end his life forever." I say, "You'll never get to see the sweet beautiful face of your son ever again. And then I'm going to point the gun at you and pull the trigger and everything you've done in your life, everyone you've loved, all of your accomplishments will be for nothing." At that point I start counting, 1… 2… I've never made it to three before the person in that exercise pulled their imaginary trigger. "Now Mary," I say, "I guess if you had to, you could take a human life, couldn't you?" The answer has always been YES.

I know this is a very graphic and dramatic illustration and I've had some participants leave shaking and visibly upset, but I needed to make the strongest impact possible, so they truly understood they have the internal power and ability to save their own lives or their loved ones if they had to. I don't do it to simply prove them wrong and me right. I do it to show them that they can kill if it comes down to them living or dying. Better to know you have it in you before it's needed than try and muster it when your life is on the line.

I hope you can do this. I hope you can summon the mental and emotional strength to put you and your family's needs before those of a killer. In the end, it may be either you or them, and maybe it will be your choice of who will survive. Consider also, in most cases at the end of the event, the killer takes his own life. If such may be the inevitable, for what reason might you decide to spare the life of the killer and possibly allow others to needlessly die as a result? For which would you forever like to feel responsible? I know my choice. NOW is the time to make yours.

Find a Weapon

If you don't regularly carry a weapon—such as a gun or a knife that you've trained with and are certified and/or capable of using (which is likely most people, especially while at work)—then now is the time to find a weapon. Arm yourself with anything you can find in your immediate vicinity to use against the attacker.

Even something as simple as a writing instrument works. When the would-be attacker comes through the door of your office, shove it into their eyeball, driving it right into their brain. It sounds barbaric, but you need to do whatever you must to make sure you are the one who is going to go home when it's over.

Other items that could easily serve as a weapon in an office or educational environment include a pair of scissors, a nail file, a leg broken off a table or a chair, a heavy coffee mug, or anything else you can reach that you could use against your attacker. A fire extinguisher could stand in for a weapon to spray or hit them with, as could a metal trash can, a keyboard, or most any other item you can pick up and use to strike the killer. Whatever you use, hit them in the most optimal area of the face or head and with the necessary force to disable them, at least temporarily if that's all you can do, so others can then attack and disable them.

Go for the eyes, the nose, or the throat. Humans have an auto response to any attack to their vision because we rely so heavily on sight. No matter what you use, if the assailant senses a threat to his eyes he will automatically do whatever he can to protect them, which means he's not pointing a gun at you and is now on the defensive.

And it doesn't matter how big the attacker is; these areas hurt when hit. Strike them with so much power that you imagine driving your weapon through their face, to the back side of the attacker's head. Fight with the strength and tenacity you'd want your child, your parent, or your sibling to fight with if he or she were in your place. Use every muscle in your body, every ounce of power you have, so you're the one who can hug your loved ones another day.

I've spoken with some corporate representatives about hiring me to give my training to their employees, but unfortunately, when I describe the VIOLENCE portion of my course, they respond with concern because their corporate culture discourages violence, or they don't want to upset some of their staff members who might be offended by encouraging violence. Guess what, people: when that killer comes through your door with the intent of wiping out everyone in that building, it's time to throw the rainbows-and-unicorns fairyland thinking out the window and start figuring out a way to survive, which may mean taking another human's life through an act of violence.

Your work culture may not accept violence in the workplace, but when someone else brings it there, you may just have to meet it head on, so be ready, willing, and able.

Swarm if You Can

If possible, swarm the killer and attack him or her as a group. While the killer may be able to overpower just one person, this becomes exponentially more difficult when faced with a whole group of people. That's why, if you can, you want to execute your violent response as a team.

To give my trainees an idea of what this looks like, I show the video of the day President Ronald Reagan was shot. Once those shots were fired, the Secret Service and other law enforcement officials instantly swarmed John Hinckley Jr. and completely incapacitated him. Yes, those officers were trained and retrained on how to act in such an event. And someday, probably sooner than you think, that training will be offered to employees, students, and others as a standard in workplaces, schools, hospitals, places of worship, and anywhere else people congregate.

This is exactly what you want to do to an active killer if you are in a group. You want to swarm him or her to gain control over the weapon, the person, and the situation to stop the threat.

If the killer has a firearm, the swarm response involves the closest and/or strongest person grabbing the muzzle of the gun or the hand holding the knife, while the rest swarm the assailant to immobilize him.

When seeking to gain control of the weapon, you should grab it with every ounce of strength you have. Imagine that it's your child, and someone is trying to take the child from you. Use brute force, and don't let it happen.

Since the muzzle directs where the bullet will go when fired, you must control it to dictate the direction of the bullet. That's why your goal is to keep the muzzle pointed down whenever possible. If fired, the bullet would hit the ground, suppressing its force or stopping it altogether, or if it does hit someone it would only be in the leg or foot if the person is in front of the shooter. If the action is carried out properly, the gunman can only get off one shot before the weapon is rendered inoperative.

It also helps if you're able to control the firing ability of the gun. After all, if no bullets can come out of it, then no one can be shot. While that doesn't necessarily remove all the danger in an active killer situation, it does help level the playing field between you and the killer.

One way to disable a handgun, which could be a revolver or semiautomatic with a visible hammer, is to grab the weapon so your thumb or finger is placed between the hammer and the frame of the gun, preventing the hammer from dropping if the trigger is pulled, so the firing pin doesn't contact the primer of the bullet.

You could also cause a jam by tightly gripping the frame and slide of a semiautomatic handgun so that, if the trigger is pulled, the slide would not have enough kinetic energy from the recoil to eject the spent round and rack a new one, causing a jam. For those of you not familiar with handgun nomenclature, just grab the gun as tightly as you can, with both hands if possible, while keeping the end of the gun pointed away from you and others, and the gun will jam, making it difficult, if not impossible, to fire again.

In the case of a would-be killer using an edged weapon or blunt object, the same principle applies. The first or most appropriate person should immediately control the weapon, while the others swarm to control the assailant.

Remember: when swarming, your first goal should be to control the weapon. Secondarily, you want to disable the killer, separating the weapon from him or her if you can.

Size Doesn't Matter

This is the point where some people may object, saying that they're too small or too weak to take on a large attacker. Another video I show in my training is of a swarm demonstration where two petite young college girls, one not even wearing shoes, surprise an attacker as he comes through the door. The first girl grabs the handgun with both hands and forces it toward the floor, while the second girl jumps on the attacker's back and they take him to the ground. You don't have to be a UFC fighter to overcome a person with a gun. You just have to have the intent and burning desire to survive.

CHAPTER TEN

EXPOSE

KEY LEARNING POINTS:

1. Before moving from a covered position and exposing yourself, *determine if you are still in danger and carefully consider all options.*

2. If you are in a secure location, *don't leave* it until you're told to do so by law enforcement or someone else you can trust.

3. When law enforcement arrives and once they tell you to come out of hiding, exit with your *hands up and palms empty* to show you are not a threat.

The last step to surviving an active killer incident is what I refer to as EXPOSE. Once you sufficiently believe the event has ended, it's time to evaluate your situation again, and if you think it's safe to do so, EXPOSE your position.

The key to exposing your position in a way that continues to help you avoid harm is to do it carefully. There are plenty of reasons for being so cautious when revealing where you have been during the incident.

For Many Reasons, Caution is the Key

One can't always be sure of the location of the killer. Because sounds tend to travel, especially down long hallways, noises like gunfire that you think are coming from one area or location may be coming from another.

Therefore, if you decide to EXPOSE your position and go on the move, instead of running away from danger, you may discover that you're running toward it. This could put you face-to-face with a killer who wouldn't have even known you were there or had access to you if you'd just stayed in place.

Secondarily, as we've discussed in previous chapters, sometimes active killers work in pairs or teams (like the husband-and-wife team in San Bernardino or the two active shooters at Columbine). This means that although one active killer may have moved past you or may be physically down, incapacitated, and unable to move, that doesn't necessarily mean the threat is over.

There could very well be another killer somewhere else in the vicinity. EXPOSE your position too early, and you could find yourself hurt or killed when you wouldn't have been if, again, you had stayed in your safe area.

A third reason to be careful when exposing your position is that law enforcement won't immediately know who is a threat and who isn't. Until they've had adequate time to sort out and process the scene, which can take hours, everyone is a suspected assailant.

This means that any sudden, unanticipated, or perceived aggressive movement on your part, or an object in your hand that could be mistaken as a weapon, is likely to provoke a response on the part of law enforcement, and when responding to an active killer incident, their primary mission is to shoot to kill. Even the most seasoned cop in a situation like this, amped on adrenaline and surrounded by carnage, might react with aggression if faced with surprise and the perception of a threat. Law enforcement's primary goal is to stop the threat, which is why you don't want to be mistaken for that threat.

Stay Put if You Can

It's best to stay put if you are in a safe place. If you're in a secure location, wait! There is absolutely no reason to rush to get out. Yes, it's likely that you're extremely scared, and yes, you probably want to get as far away from that location as possible, but the more you move around, the more you increase the potential dangers you face. And remember, these events on average last less than five minutes and almost never longer than 10. The longer you are in a safe place, the better your chances of surviving until the end of the event.

Again, although you know that you're an innocent victim in the attack, law enforcement officials don't, so you don't want to add to the confusion. The less movement the better, at least until the police issue you a directive.

Fight the Urge to Run

Again, if you are truly in a secure area, don't run if you're safe. Stay where you are until law enforcement officials tell you that it's clear to come out. It may be tempting, and your urge to flee may be growing, especially if you've been locked in your area for an extended period while officers clear the building, but you're safer if you're stationary, even if the event has ended.

Only when you're confident that the danger is over should you EXPOSE your position. Even then, you want to come out with your hands up and exit the area with law enforcement's direction, if possible. By following these few simple guidelines, you increase the likelihood that you'll survive an active killer incident.

Listen to Directives

Once law enforcement is on scene and telling you to come out, exit with your hands up and palms empty! Just as your heart is racing, and your mind is on full alert due to the situation at hand, the same is true for the responding officers. If they see something in your hand—even something innocent like a cell phone or car keys—they may mistake it for a weapon and respond accordingly.

Unless you are on your cell phone with dispatch, the best way to avoid any misinterpretations of this nature is to have absolutely nothing in your hands. The less room there is for error, the more likely it is that you'll go home as quickly and as safely as possible.

Even if you have a gun or something else to protect yourself during the incident, as soon as you encounter law enforcement, throw it away out of reach and place your hands in the air to show submission. This will help make it clear to the police that, now that they are here, you have no intention of picking up the weapon and using it. This also helps the officers know that they are safe with you, that you are not the killer, which ultimately makes you safer with them.

Whatever instructions or directives the police give to you, follow them. Even if you don't understand why they're telling you to do or not do something, understand that they may know more about the situation than you, and trust that whatever it is they're telling you to do is in your best interest.

And if they start to ask you questions, tell them what you know in as few words as possible. Although you'll likely want to share every little detail, partly because of the adrenaline racing through your veins, and partly because it would be a huge stress relief to tell your story, they only need the information that can help them determine (1) where the active killer is located, (2) what he looks like, (3) what kind of weapon he has, and (4) whether he or she is working alone. They are not there to save the dying, they are there to stop the killer from creating more casualties.

Everything else at that point is secondary, so don't worry about getting it out just yet. You'll be interviewed more in-depth as soon as the situation is under control, and you can share it all then. But for now, just share the information they need to know.

If Unsure, Contact Dispatch (911)

If you're unsure at all about whether it's safe to EXPOSE your position—maybe you haven't heard movement in a long time, yet police still haven't told you to come out—you can always call 911 and talk to a dispatcher. He or she can then advise you whether you should move from your location or not.

You should have already contacted them when the incident began and reported what was happening so that responding law enforcement knew where you were. But if not, now is an appropriate time to call. They'll know what is going on and can communicate with law enforcement on the scene to help them, and to give you the best advice.

Just make sure you speak quietly and continue to stay aware in case the situation truly hasn't ended. The less noise you make, the lower the chance the killer will be drawn to your location. Therefore, your cell phone should still be on silent as well.

Exposing your location in an active killer situation is one of the most potentially dangerous times for you, so it should always be done with care and, if possible, at law enforcement's or a dispatcher's direction.

The other thing you can do to create a more successful response is to work as a team. We covered that briefly in the last chapter when we talked about swarming, but let's go into that more in-depth because, as you'll soon learn, this one principle can be critical to surviving an active killer incident during every step.

CHAPTER ELEVEN

WORK AS A TEAM

KEY LEARNING POINTS:

1. A team mentality in active killer incidents can greatly impact your *ability to survive.*
2. Those who learn and *practice the principles* of A.L.I.V.E. as a team have the greatest chance of survival.
3. Regularly performing active shooter drills is vital to a team's ability to successfully defend themselves.

On March 18, 2017, *Harvard Business Review* (HBR) posted an article titled "How to Keep Your Team Focused and Productive During Uncertain Times." At the beginning of the piece, HBR's contributing editor and the author of the article, Amy Gallo, wrote, "Whether it's political turmoil or a reorganization at your company, employees who are concerned about their future are likely to be distracted and unproductive." Gallo goes on to say that this type of response "can be contagious", ultimately negatively affecting the whole team.

Unfortunately, the same issue can and does occur during an active killer incident, when innocent bystanders and victims become concerned about the fate of their own future. This results in feeling distracted and contributes to unproductive actions directed toward the situation, often inciting others around them to feel and respond the same way.

The only difference is that, instead of it being their jobs that are at risk, it's their lives. This makes having a cohesive and effective team response critical to everyone's survival.

Importance of a Healthy Team Mentality

If you've ever played sports, then you already understand how team performance can impact both your individual and collective team results. Work together cohesively, and you can take yourselves and your team to the championship. Work solely as individuals, without utilizing each member's strengths and contributions, and you'll be lucky to win a game or two.

Having a team mentality in active killer incidents can greatly impact your ability to survive. It involves learning how to focus on self-preservation while still acting as a team, so you'll have a solid chance of survival.

That's why, if possible, you should all do your training together as a team. When each one of you knows exactly what to do and how to respond, it reduces the need to educate everyone about what actions you should and shouldn't take, when it comes time to put that response into action. You're able to just act with minimal communication (and minimal delay) because everyone is on the same page.

There's another benefit of practicing active killer survival as a team. When you do this, there will inevitably be fewer "low-hanging fruit".

Train as a Team

Everyone should have the same training, so that each one of you is intimately familiar with the same effective active killer survival response. Everyone must learn and practice A.L.I.V.E. the same way, executing their response as a team!

Remember, in times of stress, your body and mind will default, or revert, to your training. Your body and mind will subconsciously know what to do and will help you do it, even if you learned the initial skills quite a while ago. Train as a team and you'll increase the likelihood that you'll work together like a well-oiled machine.

This training enables you to respond quickly and more effectively because you will all know what to do. It's like having a team of mechanics working on a race car or a team of doctors working together in a surgery. When each one can do his or her own part, and everyone else involved knows it, that makes everyone's chances of (and confidence in) success that much greater.

Active Killers and "Low-Hanging Fruit"

"Low-hanging fruit" in an active killer situation refers to the individuals who are the easiest to reach, thus the easiest to kill. This includes the people who didn't yet LEAVE, don't know how or where to best IMPEDE the killer's ability to get to them, or may not immediately present the obvious threat of VIOLENCE against them.

Because the active killer's goal is to take as many lives as possible in as short a time as possible, these types of people are preferred, largely because they offer the active killer the opportunity to get the most kills. They make his mission much easier.

Knowing this, if you ever find yourself in an active killer event and are inclined to assist others in that situation, you must focus on the people in your immediate vicinity who are the easiest targets, the low-hanging fruit. It's also your responsibility to not fall into that category.

Perform Active Killer Drills

One way to accomplish this type of teamwork is to regularly perform active killer drills in your workplace, hospital, school, or house of worship. Whether you're the employer or the supervisor in charge, the administrator, the principal, or the head of the church, making these drills mandatory on a quarterly or semi-annual basis could be the difference between having a building full of people who are able to successfully defend themselves against an active killer or having to tell their family members that your negligence left them unprepared.

This may sound harsh, but it's a sad reality because that's exactly what you'll be doing if you don't train your staff in active killer response, and an incident occurs. It's also one that isn't new because drills have been used for ages to help create a more effective response.

Take schools and fire drills, for instance. The National Fire Protection Association recommends that schools conduct fire drills every 30 days, at a minimum, during the school year. Why is this so important? To keep fires like the one that happened more than half a century ago (which killed 90 students) from ever happening again.

Lessons Learned from Fire

In the 1950s, schools didn't practice fire prevention by way of fire drills like they do today. So when a fire started at roughly 2:30 p.m. on December 1, 1958, at Our Lady of Angels School in Chicago, Illinois, neither students nor teachers were prepared to respond.

This resulted in widespread panic, causing some students to jump from the second floor (whether there was someone there to catch them or not) and causing others to remain right where they were, simply "praying for help". By the time all was said and done, 90 students—which was almost one-tenth of the total student body—had lost their lives, as had three nuns.

Now schools make it a priority to practice an effective response in the event of a fire starting during the school day. This only makes sense because it does happen, quite regularly, in fact; statistics provided by the Federal Emergency Management Agency (FEMA) indicate that an estimated 3,230 school fires occur each year in the United States alone. Because of nationwide mandatory fire drills in schools, not a single student has died in a school fire in over 50 years.

Doesn't it make sense, then, to practice active killer drills? These incidents are happening regularly too, so why leave your response up to chance? Plan for these types of incidents, and plan for them as a team, much the same way that you do for earthquakes, tornadoes, nuclear blasts, and any other type of disaster that serves as a possible threat to the safety of you and your staff. The difference is that whereas many of those types of events occur regionally, active shooter events can happen anywhere and anytime.

Active Killer Response Advances

Fortunately, we are seeing some advances in this arena already, such as the audible alerts, cell phone apps, or mass texts that are issued, warning everyone in the area that there is an active shooter situation. This helps initiate a team response more quickly and effectively, giving everyone in the vicinity a better chance of survival until the threat can be stopped. And as stated earlier, some law enforcement agencies now utilize text-to-911, so an emergency can be reported via text in the event the reporting party cannot call.

It's also now possible for organizations to purchase products that could prove to be invaluable in an active killer situation.

This includes the following items:

1. Door locks (yes, simple door locks can save lives)

2. Anti-intrusion devices like door blocks and locks

3. Window covers

4. First-aid and trauma kits including tourniquets and other bleeding controls

5. Camera-based security systems

6. Shot detection systems

And of course, the most effective but arguably the most controversial tool in a school, house of worship, or workplace: an actual weapon. (More and more schools, medical facilities, churches, and workplaces are beginning to approve the carrying of weapons by qualified, authorized people.)

An example of this is when, on December 29, 2019, in White Settlement, Texas, a man pulled a short stock shotgun out from under his coat and shot two men before being struck in the head from a single handgun shot fired by one of the armed church security volunteers. The gunman was instantly immobilized and therefore no longer a threat to the other 240 parishioners. It is logical that if Jack Wilson, the church member and firearms instructor who took immediate action and killed the active shooter, had not used his legally owned and concealed handgun, many more innocent people would have died that day. The entire incident lasted six seconds. This came shortly after the state legalized carrying a gun in church, prompted by the fatal shooting of 26 people during a mass shooting at the First Baptist Church in Sutherland Springs, Texas, on November 5, 2017.

By having these things in place at your organization, school, or other places you frequent, you can more effectively plan, prepare for, and respond to an active killer incident. Use these items in your regular drills so you know exactly how to utilize them in the event of an actual incident.

At the end of this book, there are some practical exercises that you can use to get started when creating your drills. Use them or feel free to create your own. Ideally, you want to plan for as many different situations as possible so you'll be more prepared should an active killer ever decide to strike where you are located. You can never be too prepared for a situation like this, so practice your responses regularly and consistently. This practice may just save your life and the lives of those around you.

CHAPTER TWELVE

RECOVERY

KEY LEARNING POINTS:

1. Incident recovery is a process that must be planned in advance.
2. The amount of resources a recovery will demand will be proportional to the size of the attack and the number of casualties.
3. Short-term recovery includes addressing immediate needs such as safety and medical assistance.
4. Long-term recovery has no set timeframe and includes support services, restoration, and reopening.
5. Post-incident scams are common, and information on how to avoid them should be given.

I n our current and ever-changing threat environment, it is important that organizations not only prepare to respond to a potential incident, but also collectively determine the processes through which the organization and its staff recover from an incident. Incidents such as those described in this book, have demonstrated that acts of violence such as active shooter incidents, can happen *anywhere and most often without warning*. Threats may be either external or internal. Although appropriate measures should be taken to protect an organization from a potential attack, it is nearly impossible to completely prevent a well-planned attack and a determined attacker. As such, if an active shooter event or other attack occurs, it is vital that organizations prepare themselves to effectively recover, taking into consideration operational and human elements.

Recovery is a continuous process that occurs over short- and long-term incremental phases. Organizations and their leaders will progress through the recovery phase at a different rate, and each will require varying degrees of assistance. In addition to assisting the psychologically harmed and physically injured, organizations must ensure the continuity of operations by returning the targeted location to its full functionality as quickly and efficiently as possible. Depending on the severity of the incident, this could range from coordinating with law enforcement's investigation of the incident, cleaning and sanitizing the scene, and replacing broken glass, to seeking a temporary alternative site in which to continue operations, providing personnel with the necessary grief counseling, addressing the media, and the inevitable litigation which will certainly follow.

Short-Term Recovery and Addressing Immediate Needs

The short-term recovery process begins immediately after an active shooter incident concludes. Its goal is to reestablish safety and mitigate the physical, psychological, and emotional impacts from the incident. For those responsible for managing the aftermath, it involves tasks that need to be implemented quickly to ensure that those affected are safe, accounted for, reunited with their families/friends, are able to retrieve their personal possessions, get proper medical and mental health care if required, and are able to receive timely information from an authoritative source about the incident and its resolution.

Preparing to address such short-term recovery issues through response policies and procedures that are regularly exercised will result in a capability to respond to such incidents in a timely, appropriate, and productive manner.

The magnitude of the incident will in large part determine how the short-term recovery process is achieved. It may be an orderly and linear sequence of steps as outlined below, or the process may be compressed or otherwise rearranged to better suit the circumstances of the incident.

Ensuring Life Safety After the Immediate Rescue

Each active killer incident has its own unique characteristics that will affect every stage of response and recovery, beginning with the short-term recovery process. The safety of victims and others initially affected by the incident are of paramount and immediate importance. Depending on any number of factors, one of the first response tasks—the evacuation process from the scene of the incident to an assembly area—may be orderly and well-planned, chaotic, or both.

Coordinate Medical Assistance

The immediate goal is to help evacuees recover sufficiently to enable them to contact family/friends, cooperate with authorities, and leave the assembly area. This will include information about survivors relocated to hospitals or other assembly areas.

- Ensure that individuals injured during the incident or evacuation are provided immediate care from responding fire and emergency medical service (EMS) personnel in the assembly area, or where circumstances dictate.

- Support efforts to transport victims unable to be treated at the scene to medical facilities

Set Up Crisis Communications Media Response

Communicating reliable and updated information about the incident, casualties, and the location and status of evacuees is of paramount importance. Ensure that such crisis communication plans are in place, including a designated crisis communications spokesperson. The crisis communication plan should include coordination with law enforcement, scripted responses to likely questions, and the designated spokesperson should be thoroughly trained to present the responses. Use the company or facility website and/or social media accounts to provide updates. Also work with local media to disseminate that same updated information. Use social media and activate a dedicated toll-free number to update information.

- Set up an officially designated toll-free telephone number as well as a social media site for continued updates on the incident and recovery, and ensure coordination with law enforcement for updated and accurate information.

- The information provided should include updated news about the situation, points of contact for emergency assistance, and other relevant measures to facilitate recovery.

- Also provide information to employees not present at the site to inform of whether or not to report for work.

- Regardless of existing crisis communication channels, ensure that evacuees' families are informed as soon as possible about their whereabouts and health status.

Provide Immediate Crisis Support

Depending on the length and severity of the incident, it may be possible to provide additional services for evacuees in the assembly areas. Some of what is described below transitions into the final stage of short-term recovery. Consider setting up a Family Assistance Center to provide:

- Information and assistance to families and friends about fatalities and survivors.

- Offer information about survivors relocated to hospitals or other assembly areas.

- Provide assistance for reunification of survivors with family or friends.

Long-Term Recovery: Restoration

The long-term recovery process begins once the assembly areas are cleared by law enforcement and the affected individuals have returned to their families and friends. The goals of long-term recovery are to help employees return to normality in their daily interactions and professional life, and to take whatever steps are necessary to return the facility and/or business to normal operations. For consideration, such restoration might include:

- Mental health counseling for the survivors and their families.

- Assistance with insurance claims and applications for unemployment insurance.

- Assistance for those with special needs with housing and/or transportation.

Reopening the Facility and Resuming Operations

Unless there is severe physical damage from an attack or other special circumstances, most facilities will reopen soon after the post-incident investigation is complete. In some cases, an alternative temporary facility may be used. Organizations should establish a reconstitution or continuity plan to restore full functionality after an incident. Considerations regarding those returning to the facility when it reopens:

- Individuals recover from traumatic incidents at their own rates. Some may be able to reestablish their normal routines and return within days, while others may need more time. Some individuals may be unable to return at all. Organizations should be prepared to accommodate an employee's progress as much as possible.

- Depending on the severity of the particular event, ensure that employees (and others affected by the incident) are aware of the need to pace themselves. Encourage them to take breaks and rest periods when possible.

- Prepare and enact continuity plans to keep operations going, if necessary. The plan may include provisions for hiring temporary staff, teleworking, and working from alternate locations.

Post-Incident Scams and Fraud

The aftermath of some active shooter incidents has seen the formation of fraudulent charities and other scams that may revictimize those affected and the general public who wish to contribute to a legitimate charity. In addition to seeking money, some of these solicitations may be "phishing" for personal information. Organizations should ensure that employees are made aware that such scams could occur. Make everyone aware of potential scams and fraud. Remind everyone:

- Fraudulent requests for donations may come from in-person, telephone, email, or social media solicitations.

- The US Internal Revenue Service maintains a list of charities that are exempt from taxation. Any charitable organization that does not appear on this list may be fraudulent. Ensure that employees are provided a link to the list of recognized charities to which they can safely donate.

- Some fraudulent charity names may resemble those of recognized charities, or they may claim an affiliation with an existing charity. Reiterate to employees the need to check website and email addresses for anomalies.

Resources

In addition to the resources listed below, organizations should consult the National Incident Management System (NIMS), which is administered by the Federal Emergency Management Agency (FEMA). NIMS provides a framework for preparation and response to any major incident, including an attack:

https://www.fema.gov/emergency-managers/nims.

Active Shooter Preparedness resources:

https://www.dhs.gov/active-shooter-preparedness

Hometown Security resources:

https://www.dhs.gov/hometown-security

Exempt Organization Select Check, IRS:

https://www.irs.gov/charities-non-profits/tax-exempt-organization-search

Helping Victims of Mass Violence & Terrorism: Planning, Response, Recovery, and Resources, DOJ-OVC, August 2015,

https://www.ovc.gov/pubs/mvt-toolkit

Guide for Developing High-Quality School Emergency
Operations Plans: A Closer Look at Active Shooters,
Department of Education:

https://rems.ed.gov/docs/REMS_K-12_Guide_508.pdf

CHAPTER THIRTEEN

IMPLEMENTING A.L.I.V.E.®
USING PRACTICAL EXERCISES

I n this chapter we will examine a number of different scenarios for you and your organization to think about, plan for, and practice when using the A.L.I.V.E. active killer response plan that you've just learned. As you go through each one, remember what you've learned:

ASSESS

Stop, breathe, process what's happening, and consider your next steps. Ask yourself: Where is the killer? Where are the exits? Can you run? If you can't run, can you IMPEDE? If you can't impede, what can you use to fight? Mentally prepare yourself to kill or be killed and be prepared to act! Call 911 as soon as you've determined the event is one of violence.

LEAVE

If you can exit the building, run as far away as possible. Also, tell everyone within earshot what you believe is happening, if possible, using a command presence to get them to LEAVE too. Leave all your belongings behind but your cell phone (which you should be on, calling 911) and a weapon, if you have one. Run in the opposite direction of the threat if that's where the most accessible exit is. The alternative is to run to a secure location (a safe room) if that is closer.

IMPEDE

Practice a lock-and-block response. Shut and lock the door if possible. If the door doesn't have a lock on it, come up with other ways to make it harder to open. Cover the windows and switch your cell phones to silent. Secure the door from entry by placing the heaviest items in the room against it first. Find a place to conceal yourself, preferably one that provides cover in addition to concealment.

VIOLENCE

Prepare for the killer's entry. Control the weapon (muzzle down) and, if possible, inhibit its firing ability. Use your own weapon or get hold of something you can use. Is swarming an option? Everyone stay on top of the attacker, and call dispatch or yell to law enforcement advising them where you are. Bottom line: attack with the intent to kill!

EXPOSE

If you are in a secure location, wait! Is the event over? Is there more than one shooter or killer? Have you received instructions from law enforcement? Are you on the phone with support, such as 911 dispatch? When you finally decide to exit, exit with your hands up and empty! Follow their instructions and tell them what you know in as few words as possible.

Creating an Exercise

Image an attack in which there is a single active killer. Now try going through the scenario and imagining two or three. Or if you could IMPEDE, and the active killer walked by in the first scenario, practice the same scenario with the active killer attempting to breach the door. Then practice it again with him or her gaining entry. The more scenarios you're prepared for, the more prepared you'll be in the event of an active killer incident.

Train as a single individual and as a team. When training in teams, think about who would be best suited for what type of response. For example, if you're impeding the active killer, are some team members more capable of moving the heavier items against the door? Or if the killer gains entry, who is going to attempt to secure the muzzle while everyone else swarms? Practice with each team member playing different roles in the scenarios so each person is more familiar and comfortable with each one.

Once you've trained with one particular scenario, change up some of the facts to create the need for different responses. This will not only better prepare you but also train your mind to consider the fact that there are many ways a scenario can go. This will help keep you more alert, so you can respond to the situation as it unfolds faster and more effectively.

Practical Exercises

Once comfortable with the fundamentals of implementing the A.L.I.V.E. active killer response, here are some practical exercises you might consider:

1. You're working at your desk and hear gunfire by the front door and people screaming. What do you do?

2. You're at work, standing by the front desk talking to a coworker, when a former employee walks in with a long gun. What do you do?

3. You're at the grocery store with your family, about ready to check out, and see a man with a gun enter the store. What do you do?

4. You're at your place of worship and, in the middle of the service, someone comes in through the rear door with a gun. What do you do?

5. You're in line at your favorite fast food place in the food court at the local mall, and you see a gunman walking down the corridor, coming toward you. What do you do?

6. You're at a parade and see a man with what appears to be explosive devices strapped to his chest walk up and stand just a few feet away. What do you do?

7. You're at a concert and see a man in front of you begin to stab other concertgoers while shouting. What do you do?

8. You're at the airport, ready to go on a nice, relaxing vacation, when you see someone attack a police officer with a long-bladed knife. What do you do?

9. You're out to eat and about to dive into your dinner when someone walks in and just starts shooting. What do you do?

10. You're at the movies with friends and, in the middle of the movie, someone walks in the side door with a gun and starts shooting. What do you do?

11. You're at the bar for an after-work drink, and someone walks in with a machete. You're sitting right by the door. What do you do?

12. You're waiting in your vehicle to pick your kids up from school and notice a man with a rifle walking toward the school. What do you do?

I hope none of these scenarios will ever happen to you. But if they do, at least you'll be prepared to deal with them as effectively as possible. You will have given yourself a chance to walk away A.L.I.V.E.!

CHAPTER FOURTEEN

CONCLUSION

S urviving an active killer incident can never be guaranteed. There's no one thing you can do that will 100% ensure that you will make it through an incident alive. However, there are many things you can do that will improve your odds dramatically, and we've covered several of them in this book.

What can you do to stay A.L.I.V.E.? Let's do a quick recap:

ASSESS

The first thing you want to do in an active killer incident is ASSESS your situation. This involves processing what's happening around you and using that information to determine your next steps. It means asking yourself questions like these:

- Where is the killer?

- Where are the exits?

- Can I run?

- If you can't run, can you IMPEDE the killer or safely conceal yourself?

- If you can't impede, what can you use to fight?

During this assessment, you must also mentally prepare yourself to kill or be killed. Remember that it's either you or the killer that will live. Make a commitment that it will be you.

While it's normal to freeze for a second or two, train yourself regularly so that you aren't left sitting there like a deer in the headlights. *Call 911 now!*

LEAVE

If possible, the best action you can take is to LEAVE the scene. Get as far away as possible, so you're not close enough to be killed or injured.

Notify others while you go. If you have a PA system or an app that is available to notify people near the event, use it. The more innocent people you can get away from the area, the more lives that will likely be saved.

Also, when leaving, use a command presence. Don't be afraid to take charge of the situation and the people in it. Talk to those around you with authority so they'll be willing to LEAVE the area safely with you. Get as far away from the threat as possible as quickly as possible, and direct others to follow you.

If you can't get out of the building, at least get safely to a secure location within that facility. Ideally, this would be a safe room with no windows, a reinforced front, and camera intercoms so insiders can see who is outside the room, but any room you can successfully prevent a killer from entering will work.

If the people with you have been through this training, they'll know where this is and will go there automatically. If not, then it may take some direction on your part to help those around you pick a safe place to wait out the event.

When you go, take only your cell phone and weapon, if you have one. More and more states are actively issuing concealed firearms licenses, so more people are carrying guns. If you have one, and your place of employment allows you to have it, take it to your safe room, keeping it hidden until you need to use it.

IMPEDE

Once you're in a safe area, IMPEDE the killer's opportunity and ability to get to you. One way to do this is to lock and block (lock the door and block it with as many things as possible, with the heaviest items closest to the door).

Your goal at this point is to become as invisible as possible by making it appear that no one is present in the room. You can do this by hiding behind objects. (Remember the principle of cover versus concealment; your best place to hide is behind something that will stop a bullet.) Additionally, cover any windows to the room so you cannot be seen IF you have time.

Effectively impeding an attacker occurs when you make yourself a "hard target". The more difficulties the killer has in reaching you, the more likely it is he will pass by you.

VIOLENCE

While locked and blocked in your safe area, arm yourself with anything you can find to injure or disable the attacker in the event he gains entry to the room. Understand that it is you or him, so you must attack the killer with the intent to kill!

If you have people with you and it's at all possible, swarm the attacker. Attack him or her as a group, control the weapon (muzzle down and keep it from firing, if you can), and disable the killer so he or she can do no further harm.

EXPOSE

If you are in a secure location, stay there until directed otherwise by law enforcement. If you must leave, once you believe the event has ended, it's time to evaluate your situation and EXPOSE your position carefully.

Because there may be additional attackers, you don't want to give your location away too soon. Plus, law enforcement won't know that you're not a bad guy, so follow all their commands as precisely as possible. This will help keep you safe until the event is over, everything is sorted out, and you can return home to your loved ones.

Be a Sheepdog

As I stated in my introduction, in Lt. Col. Dave Grossman's book, *On Combat, The Psychology and Physiology of Deadly Conflict in War and in Peace*, he writes, "Most of the people in our society are sheep. They are kind, gentle, productive creatures who can only hurt one another by accident." Grossman also goes on to explain, "Then there are the wolves and the wolves feed on the sheep without mercy… Then there are the sheepdogs and I am a sheepdog. I live to protect the flock and confront the wolf."

Remember, if you have no capacity for violence, then you are a healthy, productive citizen. You are a sheep. On the other hand, if you have a capacity for violence and no empathy for your fellow citizens, then you can be defined as an aggressive sociopath. A wolf.

But what if you have a capacity for violence and a deep love for your fellow mankind?

In this case, you are a sheepdog. A warrior. Someone who is walking the hero's path. Someone who can walk into the heart of darkness, into the universal human phobia, and walk out unscathed. Someone who can live through an active killer attack.

The World Is Changing

While some of these changes are undeniably good, some are not. One that is not is that evil people are committing more and more evil acts, making such incidents more common now than ever before.

Sadly, this situation is not likely to get better in our lifetime. With the growth of radical terror-based groups like ISIS, we will undoubtedly find more and more wolves in our society. More and more people intent on doing us harm in larger-scale attacks.

This means that we need to develop a zero-tolerance policy, one in which situations like these are not tolerated by the masses. A standard must be established so the perpetrators of

135

evil know they and their actions will not be tolerated. That they will not make victims of us; we will make victims of them. Many people are fighting hard to take us in that direction, me included, but we're not there yet.

That's why you must be as prepared as possible by adopting security and survival mindsets and practicing proactive reactionism. Instead of being on the defense by way of reaction, you must be prepared to be on the offense. You need to be diligent in your trainings by performing practical exercises and drills (like the ones at the end of this book), so that you know exactly how to respond when needed. *You need to be a sheepdog.*

You need to stay A.L.I.V.E.!

AFTERWORD

A couple weeks after the Route 91 Harvest Music Festival shooting in Las Vegas, I received an e-mail that made the thousands of hours I've spent creating, updating, and teaching my A.L.I.V.E. active shooter survival training worth every minute of effort. It read as follows:

Mr. Julian,

My name is Liz Moreno. I worked for about six years at a place called International Immunology in Murrieta, California, where you came in and gave us your active shooter survival training course. It was interesting, very informative, and I enjoyed it but never in a million years thought that I'd have to use it.

On October 1, I was in Las Vegas at the Route 91 Harvest Festival, standing at the right of the stage with my boyfriend watching Jason Aldean perform. Suddenly there was a sound like firecrackers coming from the right of us. Jason and the band ran off the stage. We turned around and two people were shot behind us, one in the face and one in the chest. Everyone immediately went forward and got down on the ground in a big pile. Right then, in that very moment when the third round of shots went off, as I was laying there attempting to cover my neck and head with my arm, your training that I had listened to years prior instantly popped into my head. I told my boyfriend, "We need to run. We cannot stay here! When he stops to reload next time, I am running!" He was hesitant at first, but I think he could tell that I was running either way. He grabbed my hand, and we ran as fast as we could, staying low and stopping to hide while shots were fired, then sprinting again in between. We ran straight to the Excalibur, where we were staying, and I sent a text to my parents at 10:14 p.m. from the lobby of Excalibur. That is how quickly we were out of there.

I truly believe taking your training is what told me to make that decision and say without a doubt that we have to run, which ultimately saved us. Had we stayed there we may have gotten shot; had we hesitated longer we could have been trampled or who knows what.

I know I'm just one of many that have had your training course, but I just wanted to let you know that I truly believe in that split second it saved our lives.

Thank you,

Liz Moreno

I met with Liz and her boyfriend shortly after receiving her letter, and we talked about her experience. She became very emotional while reliving this terrifying event, but I needed to know exactly how the training helped her so I could build on that in future trainings.

What Liz told me emphatically fueled my desire to teach as many people the A.L.I.V.E. program as quickly as I could. Liz stated that she hadn't thought about the training since attending my class three years prior, but in that moment, when she thought to herself, "This could be it; I could die today!" the training came rushing back to her like a slap in the face, and she knew exactly what she needed to do. So she ran, taking cover when the firing started again and running when it stopped.

Liz Moreno and her boyfriend, Martin Bangma (left) when they visited me at my corporate headquarters in Southern California.

As I stated in Chapter 5, people default to their level of training and remember years later how to perform CPR or the Heimlich maneuver. In this instance, that training helped save the lives of Liz and her boyfriend. Unfortunately for many who never had that training, they froze, hunkered down and took the relentless gunfire from above, waiting to die.

Please visit www.ActiveShooterSurvivalTraining.com for more information about the A.L.I.V.E. training program. You can schedule an A.L.I.V.E. training at your location by calling 833-99-ALIVE (25483) or view the online training options at www.ALIVEActiveShooter.com.

IN MEMORIAM

I wanted to provide photographs for several active shooter events, but rather than spotlighting the killers by showing pictures of them (further perpetuating their memory, which is exactly what they would want and therefore I refuse to do it), I've included photos of many of the victims and the loving memorials created in their memory. These are the people whose faces should be etched in our memories, not the culprits of these unforgiveable acts.

This list is certainly not comprehensive, and because of a lack of data available during my research, unfortunately I am unable to present more photos of the fallen. Those not shown in these pages should be remembered just as vividly as those who are.

Credit: Daily Mail

On April 20, 1999, two killers attacked Columbine High School in Littleton, Colorado, killing 13 people and wounding more than 20 others before turning their guns on themselves. At the time, this was the worst high school shooting in US history. There was speculation that the two committed the killings because they had been bullied, were members of a group of social outcasts that was fascinated by Goth culture, or had been influenced by violent video games and music.

Credit: Drew Angerer/Getty Images

IN MEMORIAM

On April 16, 2007, at 7:15 a.m., Seung-Hui Cho, 23, armed with two handguns, began shooting in a dormitory at Virginia Polytechnic Institute and State University in Blacksburg, Virginia. Two and a half hours later, he chained the doors shut in a classroom building and began shooting at the students and faculty inside. Thirty-two people were killed; 17 were wounded. The shooter committed suicide as police entered the building.

Credit: WSET/Virginia Tech

Credit: UPI/Roger L. Wollenberg

On November 5, 2009, at 1:20 p.m., Nidal Malik Hasan, 39, armed with two handguns, began shooting inside the Fort Hood Soldier Readiness Processing Center in Fort Hood, Texas. Thirteen people were killed; 32 were wounded, including one police officer. During an exchange of gunfire, the shooter was wounded and taken into custody.

Credit: AP

Credit: Wikipedia

IN MEMORIAM

On July 22, 2011, Anders Behring Breivik killed eight people and injured at least 209 more using a car bomb of mixed fertilizer and fuel oil at the executive government quarter in Oslo, Norway, before opening fire at a summer camp two hours later on Utøya, an island in Tyrifjorden, killing 69 and wounding 110.

Credit: Crime Scene Database

Credit: AP

On July 20, 2012, at 12:30 a.m., James Eagan Holmes, 24, armed with a rifle, a shotgun, and a handgun, began shooting after releasing teargas canisters in a theater at the Cinemark Century 16 movie theaters in Aurora, Colorado. Twelve people were killed; 58 were wounded.

Credit: Blogspot.com; Indy Democrat Blog

Credit: David Harpe

IN MEMORIAM

On December 14, 2012, at 9:30 a.m., Adam Lanza, 20, armed with two handguns and a rifle, shot through the secured front door to enter Sandy Hook Elementary School in Newtown, Connecticut. He killed 20 students and six adults, and he wounded two adults inside the school. Prior to the shooting, the shooter killed his mother at their home. In total, 27 people were killed; two were wounded. The shooter committed suicide after police arrived.

Credit: Time (Reuters/Rex USA)

On September 16, 2013, a lone gunman, 34-year-old Aaron Alexis, fatally shot 12 people and injured three others in a mass shooting at the headquarters of the Naval Sea Systems Command inside the Washington Navy Yard in southeast Washington, DC. The attack, which took place in the Navy Yard's Building 197, began around 8:16 a.m. and ended when Alexis was killed by police around 9:25 a.m.

Credit: CNN Compilation

Credit: Matt McClain/Washington Post

IN MEMORIAM

On May 23, 2014, at 9:27 p.m., Elliot Rodger, 22, armed with a handgun and several knives, began shooting in the first of 17 locations in Isla Vista, California. After stabbing three inside his apartment earlier that day, the shooter began driving through town, shooting from his car. He killed three and wounded seven, and he struck and wounded another seven with his vehicle. A total of six people were killed; 14 were wounded. The shooter committed suicide after being wounded during an exchange of gunfire with law enforcement.

Credit: BBC News/various sources

Credit: BBC News/various sources

149

On June 17, 2015, at 9:00 p.m., Dylann Storm Roof, 21, armed with a rifle, began shooting at a prayer service at the Emanuel African Methodist Episcopal Church in Charleston, South Carolina. Nine people were killed; no one was wounded.

Credit: USA Today/WCNC

Credit: Stephen B. Morton/AP Photo

IN MEMORIAM

On July 16, 2015, at 10:51 a.m., Mohammad Youssuf Abdulazeez, 24, armed with a rifle, began shooting at the Armed Forces Career Center in Chattanooga, Tennessee, wounding a US Marine. The shooter then drove to the Navy and Marine Reserve Center, where he killed four US Marines and wounded a law enforcement officer and a US Navy sailor who died a few days later. A total of five were killed; two were wounded, including the law enforcement officer. The shooter was killed during an exchange of gunfire with law enforcement.

Credit: Families of the Fallen Five

Credit: WRCBtv.com

On December 2, 2015, at 11:30 a.m., husband and wife Syed Rizwan Farook, 28, and Tashfeen Malik, 29, armed with two rifles, two handguns, and an explosive device, began shooting in the parking lot of the Inland Regional Center in San Bernardino, California. They moved inside the building, shooting at coworkers of one of the shooters. Fourteen people were killed; 22 were wounded. The shooters fled the scene; they were killed a few hours later during an exchange of gunfire with law enforcement.

Credit: CNN

Credit: AP

IN MEMORIAM

On June 12, 2016, at approximately 2:00 a.m., Omar Mateen, 29, armed with an assault rifle and one pistol, began shooting inside the Pulse nightclub, a dance club in Orlando, Florida. After an extended period during which the shooter barricaded himself, police entered the club and killed the shooter. Forty-nine people were killed; 53 were wounded.

Credit: DailyMail.co.uk

On October 1, 2017, Stephen Paddock opened fire on the audience of the Route 91 Harvest Country Music Festival from the 30-second floor of the Mandalay Bay Hotel and Casino in Las Vegas, Nevada, killing 58 people and wounding over 500 before killing himself just before law enforcement breached the room.

Credit: LATimes.com

Credit: Drew Angerer/Getty Images

IN MEMORIAM

On November 5, 2017, a mass shooting occurred at the First Baptist Church in Sutherland Springs, Texas, about 30 miles east of the city of San Antonio. The gunman was 26-year-old Devin Patrick Kelley of nearby New Braunfels, who killed 26 people and injured 20 others. He was shot twice by a male civilian as he exited the church. Fleeing in his SUV, Kelley crashed after a high-speed chase and was found dead with multiple gunshot wounds, including a self-inflicted shot to the head.

Credit: Reuters

Credit: Reuters

Active Shooter Incidents Ending in Suicide 2001–2016

Below is a list of active shooter incidents identified by the FBI in the United States in which the killer committed suicide. The methodology to include or exclude an incident on this list was established and articulated in the FBI's study of active shooter events released in 2014. See J. Pete Blair and Katherine W. Schweit, *A Study of Active Shooter Incidents, 2000–2013* (Washington, DC: Texas State University and Federal Bureau of Investigation, US Department of Justice, 2014).

This list is included to provide evidence of killers' predilection for ending their own lives rather than having their lives taken, at which point they would lose the sense of power and control they finally feel they have reclaimed from society and from those they believe bullied or victimized them, or otherwise deprived them of the respect they felt they deserved. *This* is why it is imperative to call 911 and get law enforcement to respond as quickly as possible. Just the sound of approaching sirens can drive an active killer to take his own life, ending the event and saving countless others from certain death.

2001

Amko Trading Store (Commerce)

On January 9, 2001, at 12:00 p.m., Ki Yung Park, 54, fatally shot his estranged wife at a convenience store they owned in Houston, Texas. Armed with two handguns, he then drove to the nearby Amko Trading Store and continued shooting. Four people were killed; no one was wounded. The shooter committed suicide when police arrived after being flagged down by a citizen.

Navistar International Corporation Factory (Commerce)

On February 5, 2001, at 9:40 a.m., William Daniel Baker, 57, armed with two rifles, a handgun, and a shotgun, began shooting coworkers in the Navistar International Corporation factory in Melrose Park, Illinois. He was supposed to report to prison the next day for stealing from Navistar. Four people were killed; four were wounded. The shooter committed suicide before police arrived.

Nu-Wood Decorative Millwork Plant, Goshen, Indiana (Commerce)

On December 6, 2001, at 2:31 p.m., Robert L. Wissman, 36, armed with a shotgun, began shooting in the Nu-Wood Decorative Millwork plant in Goshen, Indiana. He had been fired from his job that morning and returned in the afternoon to begin shooting. One person was killed; six were wounded. The shooter committed suicide before police arrived.

2002
Bertrand Products, Inc. (Commerce)

On March 22, 2002, at 8:15 a.m., William Lockey, 54, armed with a rifle and a shotgun, began shooting coworkers in the Bertrand Products, Inc., facility in South Bend, Indiana. As he attempted to flee the scene in a stolen company van, he exchanged gunfire with police, eventually committing suicide. Four people were killed; five were wounded, including three police officers.

2003
Red Lion Junior High School (Education)

On April 24, 2003, at 7:34 a.m., James Sheets, 14, armed with three handguns, shot and killed the school principal in the cafeteria at Red Lion Junior High School in Red Lion, Pennsylvania. Though others were present at the scene, the shooter committed suicide when police arrived.

Modine Manufacturing Company (Commerce)

On July 1, 2003, at 10:28 p.m., Jonathon W. Russell, 25, armed with a handgun, began shooting coworkers in the Modine Manufacturing Company building in Jefferson City, Missouri. Three people were killed; five were wounded. The shooter fled the premises and then committed suicide during an exchange of gunfire with police.

Lockheed Martin Subassembly Plant (Commerce)

On July 8, 2003, at 9:30 a.m., Douglas Paul Williams, 48, armed with a shotgun and a rifle, began shooting in the Lockheed Martin subassembly plant in Meridian, Mississippi. Six people were killed; eight were wounded. The shooter committed suicide before police arrived.

Andover Industries (Commerce)

On August 19, 2003, at 8:20 a.m., Richard Wayne Shadle, 32, armed with four handguns, began shooting in the Andover Industries facility in Andover, Ohio, after his boss threatened to fire him. One person was killed; two were wounded. The shooter committed suicide before police arrived.

2004

ConAgra Plant (Commerce)

On July 2, 2004, at 5:00 p.m., Elijah J. Brown, 21, armed with a handgun, began shooting employees in the ConAgra plant in Kansas City, Kansas. He had been laid off due to a production slowdown but was rehired six weeks prior to the incident. Six people were killed; two were wounded. The shooter committed suicide before police arrived.

Radio Shack, Gateway Mall (Commerce)

On November 18, 2004, at 6:45 p.m., Justin Michael Cudar, 25, armed with a handgun, began shooting in the Radio Shack at the Gateway Mall in Saint Petersburg, Florida. Two were killed; one was wounded. The shooter committed suicide before police arrived.

2005

DaimlerChrysler's Toledo North Assembly Plant (Commerce)

On January 26, 2005, at 8:34 p.m., Myles Wesley Meyers, 54, armed with a shotgun, returned from his lunch break and began shooting in DaimlerChrysler's Toledo North Assembly plant in Toledo, Ohio. He took a woman hostage before beginning to shoot at his coworkers. One person was killed; two were wounded. The shooter committed suicide before police arrived.

Living Church of God (House of Worship)

On March 12, 2005, at 12:51 p.m., Terry M. Ratzmann, 44, armed with a handgun, began shooting during a Living Church of God service at the Sheraton Hotel in Brookfield, Wisconsin. Seven people were killed; four were wounded. The shooter committed suicide before police arrived.

Red Lake High School and Residence (Education)

On March 21, 2005, at 2:49 p.m., Jeffery James Weise, 16, armed with a shotgun and two handguns, began shooting at Red Lake High School in Red Lake, Minnesota. Before the incident at the school, the shooter fatally shot his grandfather, who was a police officer, and another individual at their home. He then took his grandfather's police equipment, including guns and body armor, to the school. A total of nine people were killed, including an unarmed security guard, a teacher, and five students; six students were wounded. The shooter committed suicide during an exchange of gunfire with police.

Parking Lots, Philadelphia, Pennsylvania (Open Space)

On October 7, 2005, at 10:13 a.m., Alexander Elkin, 45, armed with a handgun, shot two people in different parking lots in Philadelphia, Pennsylvania. He shot his ex-wife and then drove with her body in the car to kill her friend at another location. An off-duty police officer witnessed the shooting and flagged down an on-duty police officer to pursue the shooter. After an exchange of gunfire with police, the shooter retreated to his car, where he committed suicide. Two people were killed; no one was wounded.

2006

Santa Barbara US Postal Processing and Distribution Center (Government/Commerce)

On January 30, 2006, at 7:15 p.m., former postal worker Jennifer San Marco, 44, armed with a handgun, began shooting at her previous place of employment, the Santa Barbara US Postal Processing and Distribution Center in Goleta, California. Six people were killed; no one was wounded. The shooter committed suicide before police arrived.

Residence, Capitol Hill Neighborhood, Seattle, Washington (Residence)

On March 25, 2006, at 7:03 a.m., Kyle Aaron Huff, 28, armed with a handgun, a shotgun, and a rifle, began shooting at a rave after-party in the Capitol Hill neighborhood of Seattle, Washington. Six people were killed; two were wounded. The shooter committed suicide as police confronted him.

Essex Elementary School and Two Residences (Education)

On August 24, 2006, at 1:55 p.m., Christopher Williams, 26, armed with a handgun, shot at various locations in Essex, Vermont. He began by fatally shooting his ex-girlfriend's mother at her home and then drove to Essex Elementary School, where his ex-girlfriend was a teacher. He did not find her, but as he searched, he killed one teacher and wounded another. He then fled to a friend's home, where he wounded one person. A total of two people were killed; two were wounded. The shooter also attempted suicide by shooting himself twice but survived and was apprehended when police arrived at the scene.

West Nickel Mines School (Education)

On October 2, 2006, at 10:30 a.m., Charles Carl Roberts IV, 32, armed with a rifle, a shotgun, and a handgun, began shooting at the West Nickel Mines School in Bart Township, Pennsylvania. After the shooter entered the building, he ordered all males and adults out of the room. After a 20-minute standoff, he began firing. The shooter committed suicide as the police began to breach the school through a window. Five people were killed; five were wounded.

2007

ZigZag Net, Inc. (Commerce)

On February 12, 2007, at 8:00 p.m., Vincent Dortch, 44, armed with a rifle and a handgun, began shooting during a ZigZag Net, Inc. board meeting at the Naval Business Center in Philadelphia, Pennsylvania. The shooter had scheduled the board meeting to discuss a financial dispute with other board members. Three people were killed; one was wounded. The shooter committed suicide after firing at the police.

Kenyon Press (Commerce)

On March 5, 2007, at 9:00 a.m., Alonso Jose Mendez, 68, armed with a handgun, began shooting at his coworkers in the Kenyon Press facility in Signal Hill, California. No one was killed; three were wounded. The shooter committed suicide before police arrived.

Virginia Polytechnic Institute and State University (Education)

On April 16, 2007, at 7:15 a.m., Seung-Hui Cho, 23, armed with two handguns, began shooting in a dormitory at Virginia Polytechnic Institute and State University in Blacksburg, Virginia. Two and a half hours later, he chained the doors shut in a classroom building and began shooting at the students and faculty inside. Thirty-two people were killed; 17 were wounded. In addition, six students were injured jumping from a second-floor classroom and were not included in other reported injury totals. The shooter committed suicide as police entered the building.

Residence, Latah County Courthouse, and First Presbyterian Church (Residence/Government/ House of Worship)

On May 19, 2007, around 11:00 p.m., Jason Kenneth Hamilton, 36, armed with two rifles, began shooting outside the Latah County Courthouse in Moscow, Idaho, killing one police officer and wounding two people, including another police officer. He then fled to the First Presbyterian Church across the street and continued shooting, killing a citizen and wounding two people, including another police officer. Before driving to the courthouse, he fatally shot his wife in their residence. A total of three people were killed; three were wounded. The shooter committed suicide after police arrived.

Residence in Crandon, Wisconsin (Residence)

On October 7, 2007, at 2:45 a.m., Tyler Peterson, 20, a sheriff's deputy armed with a rifle, began shooting during a party at his ex-girlfriend's house in Crandon, Wisconsin. Six people were killed, including his ex-girlfriend; one was wounded. The shooter later committed suicide during an exchange of gunfire with police.

Am-Pac Tire Pros (Commerce)

On October 8, 2007, at 7:30 a.m., Robert Becerra, 29, armed with a handgun, began shooting at customers and employees of Am-Pac Tire Pros in Simi Valley, California. One person was killed; two were wounded. The shooter committed suicide before police arrived.

SuccessTech Academy (Education)

On October 10, 2007, at 1:02 p.m., Asa Halley Coon, 14, armed with two handguns, began shooting at SuccessTech Academy in Cleveland, Ohio. No one was killed; four were wounded. The shooter committed suicide before police arrived.

Von Maur, Westroads Mall (Commerce)

On December 5, 2007, at 1:42 p.m., Robert Arthur Hawkins, 19, armed with a rifle, began shooting as he exited the elevator on the third floor of the Von Maur department store in the Westroads Mall in Omaha, Nebraska. Eight people were killed; four were wounded. The shooter committed suicide before police arrived.

Youth with a Mission Training Center / New Life Church (House of Worship)

On December 9, 2007, at 12:29 a.m., Matthew John Murray, 24, armed with a rifle, two handguns, and smoke bombs, entered the Youth with a Mission Training Center in Arvada, Colorado, and began shooting. Two people were killed; two were wounded. He then walked seven miles overnight to the New Life Church in Colorado Springs, Colorado, and began shooting again. Two additional people were killed there; three more were wounded. The shooter committed suicide after being shot by church security. A total of four people were killed; five were wounded.

2008

Louisiana Technical College (Education)

On February 8, 2008, at 8:35 a.m., Latina Williams, 23, armed with a handgun, began shooting in a second-floor classroom at Louisiana Technical College in Baton Rouge, Louisiana. She fired six rounds, then reloaded and committed suicide before police arrived. Two people were killed; no one was wounded.

Cole Hall Auditorium, Northern Illinois University (Education)

On February 14, 2008, at 3:00 p.m., Steven Phillip Kazmierczak, 27, armed with a shotgun and three handguns, began shooting in the Cole Hall Auditorium at Northern Illinois University in DeKalb, Illinois. He had attended graduate school at the university. Five were killed; 16 were wounded, including three who were injured as they fled. The shooter committed suicide before police arrived.

Wendy's Fast Food Restaurant (Commerce)

On March 3, 2008, at 12:15 p.m., Alburn Edward Blake, 60, armed with a handgun, began shooting in a Wendy's restaurant in West Palm Beach, Florida. One person was killed; four were wounded. The shooter committed suicide before police arrived.

Atlantis Plastics Factory (Commerce)

On June 25, 2008, at 12:00 a.m., Wesley Neal Higdon, 25, armed with a handgun, began firing at his coworkers in the Atlantis Plastics factory in Henderson, Kentucky. Prior to the incident, he was reprimanded by a supervisor for having an argument with a coworker and was escorted from the plant. He returned a brief time later and began shooting. Five people were killed; one was wounded. The shooter committed suicide before police arrived.

2009

The Zone Nightclub (Commerce)

On January 24, 2009, at 10:37 p.m., Erik Salvador Ayala, 24, armed with a handgun, began shooting at a crowd outside the Zone, an under-21 nightclub in Portland, Oregon, and then shot himself before police arrived. He died in the hospital two days later. Two people were killed; seven were wounded.

Coffee and Geneva Counties, Alabama (Open Space)

On March 10, 2009, at 4:00 p.m., Michael Kenneth McLendon, 28, armed with a rifle, killed five family members at various locations as he traveled through Coffee and Geneva Counties in southeast Alabama and continued shooting. A total of 10 people were killed; one police officer was wounded. During an exchange of gunfire with police, the shooter committed suicide.

American Civic Association Center (Commerce)

On April 3, 2009, at 10:31 a.m., Linh Phat Voong, aka Jiverly Wong, 41, armed with two handguns, began shooting in the American Civic Association Center in Binghamton, New York. He had previously taken classes at the center. The shooter blocked the back door of the building with his car and then entered through the front door. Thirteen people were killed; four were wounded. The shooter committed suicide before police arrived.

Larose-Cut Off Middle School (Education)

On May 18, 2009, at 9:00 a.m., Justin Doucet, 15, armed with a handgun, fired once at a teacher at Larose-Cut Off Middle School in Cut Off, Louisiana, then went to the bathroom and shot himself. He died a week later. No one was killed or wounded.

LA Fitness (Commerce)

On August 4, 2009, at 7:56 p.m., George Sodini, 48, armed with three handguns, began shooting in an LA Fitness aerobics class at the Great Southern Shopping Center in Collier Township, Pennsylvania. He entered the gym, removed his guns from his gym bag, and began firing in the aerobics studio. Three people were killed; nine were wounded. The shooter committed suicide before police arrived.

Legacy Metrolab in Tualatin, Oregon (Commerce)

On November 10, 2009, at 11:49 a.m., Robert Beiser, 39, armed with a handgun, a rifle, and a shotgun, began firing in the Legacy Metrolab in Tualatin, Oregon, his wife's place of employment. One week earlier, his wife had filed for divorce. His wife was killed; two were wounded. The shooter committed suicide before police arrived.

2010

ABB Plant (Commerce)

On January 7, 2010, at 6:30 a.m., Timothy Hendron, 51, armed with two handguns, a shotgun, and a rifle, began shooting at his coworkers in the parking lot at the ABB Plant in Saint

Louis, Missouri, before moving into the building. He was a party in a pending lawsuit against his employer regarding the company's retirement plan. Three people were killed; five were wounded. The shooter committed suicide before police arrived.

Farm King Store, Macomb, Illinois (Commerce)

On February 3, 2010, at 12:45 p.m., Jonathan Joseph Labbe, 19, armed with a rifle, began shooting inside a Farm King store in Macomb, Illinois. Eight people barricaded themselves in the office and remained hidden until police arrived. No one was killed or wounded. The shooter committed suicide after police arrived.

Ohio State University, Maintenance Building (Education)

On March 9, 2010, at 3:30 a.m., Nathaniel Alvin Brown, 50, armed with two handguns, began shooting in the maintenance building at Ohio State University in Columbus, Ohio. He had just been fired for allegedly lying on his job application. One person was killed; one was wounded. The shooter committed suicide before police arrived.

Parkwest Medical Center, Knoxville, Tennessee (Health Care)

On April 19, 2010, at 4:30 p.m., Abdo Ibssa, 38, armed with a handgun, began shooting in the Parkwest Medical Center in Knoxville, Tennessee. He had been distressed over the outcome of his recent surgery and was trying to find his doctor, who he believed had implanted a microchip in him. When he was unable to find the doctor, he moved to the emergency room and began shooting. One person was killed; two were wounded. The shooter committed suicide before police arrived.

Boulder Stove and Flooring (Commerce)

On May 17, 2010, at 11:05 a.m., Robert Phillip Montgomery, 53, armed with a handgun, began shooting at the owners in the back office of Boulder Stove and Flooring in Boulder, Colorado. Two people were killed; no one was wounded. The shooter committed suicide before police arrived.

Yoyito Café (Commerce)

On June 6, 2010, at 10:00 p.m., Gerardo Regalado, 37, armed with a handgun, began shooting in Yoyito Café in Hialeah, Florida, where his estranged wife was employed. Four people were killed, including his estranged wife; three were wounded. The shooter fled the scene and committed suicide several blocks away.

Emcore Corporation (Commerce)

On July 12, 2010, at 9:30 a.m., Robert Reza, 37, armed with a handgun, began shooting in the Emcore Corporation building in Albuquerque, New Mexico, his girlfriend's place of employment. After confronting her, he began shooting throughout the building. Two people were killed; four were wounded, including his girlfriend. The shooter committed suicide once corporate security arrived.

Hartford Beer Distribution Center (Commerce)

On August 3, 2010, at 7:00 a.m., Omar Sheriff Thornton, 34, armed with two handguns, began shooting at his coworkers in the Hartford Beer Distribution Center in Manchester, Connecticut. He had been asked to quit for stealing beer from the warehouse. Eight people were killed; two were wounded. The shooter committed suicide after police arrived.

AmeriCold Logistics (Commerce)

On September 22, 2010, at 9:54 p.m., Akouch Kashoual, 26, armed with a handgun, began shooting at his coworkers in the break room of the AmeriCold Logistics plant in Crete, Nebraska. No one was killed; three were wounded. The shooter committed suicide before police arrived.

Gainesville, Florida (Open Space)

On October 4, 2010, at 4:00 p.m., Clifford Louis Miller Jr., 24, armed with a handgun, began shooting as he drove around Gainesville, Florida. One person, his father, was killed; five were wounded. The shooter committed suicide in a friend's driveway 13 minutes after the shooting began.

Panama City School Board Meeting (Education)

On December 14, 2010, at 2:14 p.m., Clay Allen Duke, 56, armed with a handgun, began shooting during a school board meeting in the Nelson Administrative Building in Panama City, Florida. The shooter's wife had previously been employed by the school district. After allowing several people to leave the room, the shooter fired in the direction of board members. No one was killed or wounded. The shooter committed suicide after being shot by the school district's armed security officer.

2011

Millard South High School in Omaha, Nebraska (Education)

On January 5, 2011, at 12:44 p.m., Richard L. Butler Jr., 17, armed with a handgun, began shooting in Millard South High School in Omaha, Nebraska. Earlier that day, the assistant principal had suspended the shooter for allegedly driving his car onto the football field. The assistant principal was killed; the principal was wounded. The shooter committed suicide after fleeing the site of the shooting.

International House of Pancakes (Commerce)

On September 6, 2011, at 8:58 a.m., Eduardo Sencion, also known as Eduardo Perez-Gonzalez, 32, armed with a rifle, began shooting in an International House of Pancakes in Carson City, Nevada. Three members of the US Air National Guard were killed, and two were wounded. In total, four people were killed; seven were wounded. The shooter committed suicide before police arrived.

Southern California Edison Corporate Office Building (Commerce)

On December 16, 2011, at 1:30 p.m., Andre Turner, 51, armed with a handgun, began shooting at his coworkers in a Southern California Edison corporate office building in Irwindale, California. Turner had just been told he would not receive a Christmas bonus and might be laid off. Two people were killed; two were wounded. The shooter committed suicide before police arrived.

2012

McBride Lumber Company (Commerce)

On January 13, 2012, at 6:10 a.m., Ronald Dean Davis, 50, armed with a shotgun, began shooting at his coworkers at McBride Lumber Company in Star, North Carolina. Three people were killed, one was wounded. The shooter shot himself at another location and later died in the hospital.

Café Racer (Commerce)

On May 30, 2012, at 10:52 a.m., Ian Lee Stawicki, 40, armed with two handguns, began shooting inside Café Racer in Seattle, Washington, which he had been banned from entering because of previous incidents. He then fled to a parking lot, where he killed a woman to steal her car. Five people were killed; no one was wounded. The shooter committed suicide at another location.

Sikh Temple of Wisconsin (House of Worship)

On August 5, 2012, at 10:25 a.m., Wade Michael Page, 40, armed with a handgun, began shooting outside the Sikh Temple of Wisconsin in Oak Creek, Wisconsin, and then moved inside and continued to shoot. The shooter exited the building and confronted the responding police officer, wounding him. He then fired on a second responding police officer, who returned fire and wounded the shooter. Six people were killed; four were wounded, including one police officer. The shooter committed suicide after being shot in the stomach by the second responding officer.

Pathmark Supermarket, Old Bridge, New Jersey (Commerce)

On August 31, 2012, at 4:00 a.m., Terence Tyler, 23, armed with a rifle and a handgun, began shooting at his coworkers in a Pathmark supermarket in Old Bridge, New Jersey. He returned after his shift dressed in military fatigues and carrying his weapons. He shot at a coworker outside the store, who ran inside and locked the door, warning other employees. The shooter gained entry to the store by shooting out the lock. Two people were killed; no one was wounded. The shooter committed suicide before police arrived.

Accent Signage Systems (Commerce)

On September 27, 2012, at 4:35 p.m., Andrew John Engeldinger, 36, armed with a handgun, began shooting in the Accent Signage Systems facility in Minneapolis, Minnesota. The shooter had just been fired from the company. Six people were killed; two were wounded. The shooter committed suicide before police arrived.

Las Dominicanas M&M Hair Salon (Commerce)

On October 18, 2012, at 11:04 a.m., Bradford Ramon Baumet, 36, armed with a handgun, began shooting in the Las Dominicanas M&M Hair Salon in Casselberry, Florida. The shooter had been served earlier that month with a domestic-violence court order involving his ex-girlfriend, who managed the salon. Three people were killed; his ex-girlfriend was wounded. The shooter committed suicide at another location.

Azana Day Salon (Commerce)

On October 21, 2012, at 11:09 a.m., Radcliffe Franklin Haughton, 45, armed with a handgun, began shooting in the Azana Day Salon in Brookfield, Wisconsin, his estranged wife's place of employment. Three were killed, including his estranged wife; four were wounded. The shooter committed suicide before police arrived.

Valley Protein (Commerce)

On November 6, 2012, at 8:15 a.m., Lawrence Jones, 42, armed with a handgun, began shooting at his coworkers in the Valley Protein processing plant in Fresno, California. The shooting took place midway through his shift. Two people were killed; two were wounded. The shooter committed suicide before police arrived.

Clackamas Town Center Mall (Commerce)

On December 11, 2012, at 3:25 p.m., Jacob Tyler Roberts, 22, armed with a rifle, began shooting at people waiting to see Santa Claus in the Clackamas Town Center Mall in Happy Valley, Oregon. Two people were killed; one was wounded. The shooter committed suicide before police arrived.

Sandy Hook Elementary School and Residence (Education/Residence)

On December 14, 2012, at 9:30 a.m., Adam Lanza, 20, armed with two handguns and a rifle, shot through the secured front door to enter Sandy Hook Elementary School in Newtown, Connecticut. He killed 20 students and six adults, and he wounded two adults inside the school. Prior to the shooting, the shooter killed his mother at their home. In total, 27 people were killed; two were wounded. The shooter committed suicide after police arrived.

2013

Osborn Maledon Law Firm (Commerce)

On January 30, 2013, at 10:45 a.m., Arthur Douglas Harmon III, 70, armed with a handgun, began shooting during a mediation session at the Osborn Maledon law firm in Phoenix, Arizona. Two people were killed; one was wounded. The shooter later committed suicide at another location.

Lake Butler, Florida (Open Space)

On August 24, 2013, at 9:20 a.m., Hubert Allen Jr., 72, armed with a rifle and a shotgun, began shooting at his coworkers from Pritchett Trucking, Inc., as he drove around Lake Butler, Florida. He then returned home, where he committed suicide. Two people were killed; two were wounded.

Sparks Middle School (Education)

On October 21, 2013, at 7:16 a.m., Jose Reyes, 12, armed with a handgun, began shooting outside Sparks Middle School in Sparks, Nevada. A teacher was killed when he confronted the shooter; two people were wounded. The shooter committed suicide before police arrived.

Arapahoe High School (Education)

On December 13, 2013, at 12:30 p.m., Karl Halverson Pierson, 18, armed with a shotgun, machete, and three Molotov cocktails, began shooting in the hallways of Arapahoe High School in Centennial, Colorado. As he moved through the school and into the library, he fired one additional round and lit a Molotov cocktail, throwing it into a bookcase and causing minor damage. One person was killed; no one was wounded. The shooter committed suicide as a school resource officer approached him.

Renown Regional Medical Center (Health Care)

On December 17, 2013, at 2:00 p.m., Alan Oliver Frazier, 51, armed with a shotgun and two handguns, began shooting in the Renown Regional Medical Center in Reno, Nevada. One person was killed; two were wounded. The shooter committed suicide at the scene after police arrived.

2014

The Mall in Columbia (Commerce)

On January 25, 2014, at 11:15 a.m., Darion Marcus Aguilar, 19, armed with a shotgun and explosive devices, began shooting in the Mall in Columbia, Maryland, first in a retail store, then in the open mall. Two store employees were killed; five mall patrons were wounded. One person was shot in the ankle, and four others suffered other medical emergencies. The shooter committed suicide before law enforcement arrived.

Fort Hood Army Base, Texas (Government)

On April 2, 2014, at 4:00 p.m., Ivan Antonio Lopez-Lopez, 34, armed with a handgun, began shooting inside an administrative office on the Fort Hood Army Base in Texas. The active-duty soldier then moved (sometimes on foot, other times in a vehicle) from one location to another, firing inside and outside buildings. Three soldiers were killed; 12 were wounded. The shooter committed suicide after being confronted by a military law enforcement officer.

Federal Express (Commerce)

On April 29, 2014, at 5:50 a.m., Geddy Lee Kramer, 19, armed with a shotgun and explosive devices, began shooting at coworkers in a Federal Express sorting facility in Kennesaw, Georgia. He shot an unarmed security guard at the entrance control point and made his way into the facility, where he shot five more. No one was killed; six were wounded. The shooter committed suicide before law enforcement arrived.

Residence and Construction Site in Jonesboro, Arkansas (Residence/Open Area)

On May 3, 2014, at 1:00 p.m., Porfirio Sayago-Hernandez, 40, armed with a handgun, began shooting at a friend's home in Jonesboro, Arkansas, killing two people and wounding four. The shooter then drove to a nearby construction site and killed one. A total of three people were killed; four were wounded. The shooter fled the scene and committed suicide at another location.

Multiple Locations, Isla Vista, California (Open Space)

On May 23, 2014, at 9:27 p.m., Elliot Rodger, 22, armed with a handgun and several knives, began shooting in the first of 17 locations in Isla Vista, California. After stabbing three inside his apartment earlier that day, he began driving through town, shooting from his car. A total of six people were killed; 14 were wounded. The shooter committed suicide after being wounded during an exchange of gunfire with law enforcement.

Cici's Pizza and Walmart (Commerce)

On June 8, 2014, at 11:20 a.m., husband and wife Jerad Dwain Miller, 31, and Amanda Renee Miller, 22, each armed with a handgun (and one with a shotgun), began shooting at Cici's Pizza in Las Vegas, Nevada, killing two law enforcement officers who were having lunch. The shooters took the officers' weapons and ammunition and fled to a nearby Walmart, where they killed an armed citizen who tried to intervene. Three were killed; no one was wounded. The male shooter was killed in an exchange of gunfire with law enforcement; the female shooter committed suicide during an exchange of gunfire with law enforcement.

Reynolds High School (Education)

On June 10, 2014, at 8:05 a.m., Jared Michael Padgett, 15, armed with a handgun and a rifle, began shooting inside the boys' locker room at Reynolds High School in Portland, Oregon. One student was killed; one teacher was wounded. The shooter committed suicide after law enforcement arrived.

United Parcel Service (Commerce)

On September 23, 2014, at 9:20 a.m., Kerry Joe Tesney, 45, armed with a handgun, began shooting in a UPS shipping facility in Birmingham, Alabama, from which he had recently been fired. Two supervisors were killed; no one was wounded. The shooter committed suicide before law enforcement arrived.

Marysville-Pilchuck High School (Education)

On October 24, 2014, at 10:39 a.m., Jaylen Ray Fryberg, 15, armed with a handgun, began shooting in the cafeteria of Marysville-Pilchuck High School in Marysville, Washington. Four students were killed, including the shooter's cousin; three were wounded, including one who injured himself while fleeing the scene. The shooter, when confronted by a teacher, committed suicide before law enforcement arrived.

2015

Melbourne Square Mall (Commerce)

On January 17, 2015, at 9:31 a.m., Jose Garcia-Rodriguez, 57, armed with three handguns, began shooting at his wife's workplace, Scotto Pizza, in Melbourne Square Mall in Melbourne, Florida. One person was killed; the shooter's wife was wounded. The shooter committed suicide before law enforcement arrived.

Sioux Steel Pro-Tec (Commerce)

On February 12, 2015, at 2:00 p.m., Jeffrey Scott DeZeeuw, 51, armed with a handgun, began shooting at coworkers at a steel mill in Lennox, South Dakota. One coworker was killed; two were wounded, including one who tried to intervene. The shooter fled the scene and committed suicide at another location.

Walmart Supercenter (Commerce)

On May 26, 2015, at 1:00 a.m., Marcell Travon Willis, 21, an active-duty US airman, armed with a handgun, began shooting at a Walmart Supercenter in Grand Forks, North Dakota. One store employee was killed; one store employee was wounded. The shooter committed suicide before law enforcement arrived.

Grand 16 Theatre (Commerce)

On July 23, 2015, at 7:15 p.m., John Russell Houser, 59, armed with a handgun, began shooting moviegoers in the Grand 16 Theatre in Lafayette, Louisiana. Two people were killed; nine were wounded. The shooter committed suicide after law enforcement arrived.

Syverud Law Office and Miller-Meier Limb and Brace, Inc. (Commerce)

On October 26, 2015, at 1:56 p.m., Robert Lee Mayes Jr., 40, armed with a handgun, began shooting at his estranged wife's workplace, Syverud Law Office, in Davenport, Iowa. The shooter then drove to Miller-Meier Limb and Brace, Inc., in nearby Bettendorf, where his estranged wife's father and an acquaintance were employed, and continued shooting. No one was killed; two were wounded. The shooter committed suicide after law enforcement arrived.

2016
Knight Transportation Building (Commerce)

On May 4, 2016, at approximately 8:45 a.m., Marion Guy William, 65, armed with a shotgun and a handgun, began shooting as he entered the Knight Transportation building in Harris County, Texas. The shooter, who had been fired from the company two weeks prior, killed a former coworker and then committed suicide. Two former coworkers were struck by shrapnel. One person was killed; two were wounded.

The Plaza Live Theater (Commerce)

On June 10, 2016, at approximately 10:24 p.m., Kevin James Loibl, 27, armed with two handguns and a hunting knife, approached and fatally shot singer Christina Grimmie as she signed autographs during a meet-and-greet session after a concert at the Plaza Live Theater in Orlando, Florida. The suspect committed suicide after being tackled by the singer's brother. One person was killed; no one was wounded. Though only one person was killed, the assailant had multiple weapons, so it is believed he intended to continue killing.

2017

Route 91 Harvest Music Festival (Open Space)

On October 1, 2017, millionaire businessman Stephen Paddock opened fire on the audience of the Route 91 Harvest Festival from the 30-second floor of the Mandalay Bay Hotel and Casino in Las Vegas, Nevada, killing 58 people and wounding over 500 more. Paddock committed suicide when law enforcement determined which room he was in and was about to breach the door.

First Baptist Church (House of Worship)

On Sunday, November 5, 2017, another horrifying mass killing occurred that took the lives of 26 people, including children, while they worshipped at the First Baptist Church in Sutherland Springs, Texas. The shooter, 26-year-old Devin Kelley, a dishonorably discharged US Air Force service member with a history of violence against his family members and animals, entered the church and began randomly shooting. The shooter committed suicide after being shot and chased by a private citizen.

INDEX

9

911, **ix**, **84**, **91**, **101**, **120**, **127**, **141**, **142**, **147**, **171**

A

A.L.I.V.E., **v**, **vi**, **viii**, **x**, **71**, **106**, **122**, **124**, **140**, **144**, **151**, **152**, **154**, **155**
Aaron Hancey, 6
ABB Plant, 188, 189
active killer, 11, 14, 91, 106, 121, 125, 142
active shooter, **i**, **ii**, **i**, **v**, **vi**, **1**, **3**, **4**, **10**, **12**, **17**, **18**, **20**, **22**, **23**, **24**, **25**, **26**, **27**, **28**, **31**, **32**, **33**, **34**, **35**, **36**, **37**, **39**, **40**, **43**, **44**, **45**, **46**, **53**, **54**, **57**, **60**, **61**, **64**, **69**, **70**, **71**, **78**, **84**, **95**, **101**, **127**, **130**, **131**, **137**, **152**, **156**
Active Shooter, **ii**, **v**, **vi**, **v**, **2**, **10**, **17**, **18**, **23**, **37**, **40**, **45**, **58**, **71**, **75**, **138**, **171**
active shooters, 18, 25, 42, 43, 44, 52, 55, 61, 116
Al Qaeda, 52
Alpine High School, 42
American Civic Association Center, 186
Amko Trading Store, 171, 172
Am-Pac Tire Pros, 182
Andover Industries, 175
AR-15 rifle, 89
Arkansas, 201, 202

B

bankruptcy, 45
Bertrand Products, 173
Bill Husfelt, 50
Blacksburg, Virginia, 26, 158, 181
bombs, 4, 5, 183
Boulder, 190
bullet, 5, 94, 102, 112, 113, 148
bullets, 89, 113
bullying, 4

C

California, **i**, **iii**, **13**, **17**, **35**, **55**, **152**, **154**, **164**, **167**, **178**, **180**, **182**, **193**, **198**, **202**
CEO, 2, 17
Charleston, 53, 165
Chicago, **126**
church, vii, 125, 170, 183, 207
Cinemark Century 16, 21, 26, 161
Cole Hall Auditorium, 185
Colorado, ii, 3, 18, 21, 26, 49, 51, 95, 157, 161, 183, 190, 200
Columbine, 1, 2, 4, 7, 8, 19, 44, 103, 116, 157
Columbine High School, 2, 157
conceal, 9, 94
Connecticut, ii, 33, 39, 51, 162, 191, 199
CPR, 69, 155

ABOUT THE AUTHOR

Michael Julian, the creator of the A.L.I.V.E. Active Shooter Survival Training Program, began his training and assisted his father Ron Julian, founder of the parent company National Business Investigations (NBI), at the age of 16. He majored in Administration of Justice in college where he was inducted into the Phi Theta Kappa International Scholastic Order for Academic Achievement.

He began working full time for NBI in 1990, specializing in surveillance operations and continued his education by completing the California Department of Justice Reserve Law Enforcement Academy and studying advanced surveillance techniques from the National Association of Investigative Specialists.

Michael joined the California Association of Licensed Investigators (CALI) in 1995, where he served as a district governor, on the Legislation and Technology Committees, Education & Training Task Force, Board of Directors as the Vice President of Administrative Services for five terms, and as president in 2012 and 2013.

Michael created MPS Security & Protection, the personal and asset protection division of NBI in 2003 to satisfy the increase in demand for executive-level and facility security services. He is licensed in multiple states as a private investigator and security professional, is a graduate of the Executive Protection Institute and Executive Security International, and board director or member of several national and international security associations.

Michael's security training includes behavioral threat assessment, active shooter survival, executive and asset protection, self-defense, defensive and evasive driving, close protection, aviation security, protective surveillance and counter surveillance, and covert protection. Besides Active Shooter, he teaches training courses in Executive and Asset Protection throughout the United States, and is a trusted security consultant for numerous organizations, teaching workplace violence identification and reaction, and active shooter survival, and featured security expert for ABC Channel 7 News.

A.L.I.V.E. was created in 2014 when Michael began teaching his Active Shooter Survival philosophy throughout the United States. His book on the subject, *10 Minutes to Live: Surviving an Active Shooter Using A.L.I.V.E.* was published in 2017, and the online version of the A.L.I.V.E. Training Program was launched in 2019 and is now part of the corporate security training program for companies throughout the world. In mid-2019 the first A.L.I.V.E. Instructor Certification Course was held in Southern California, creating several new, qualified instructors to present the program, who now teach A.L.I.V.E. throughout the world.

Michael is a keynote speaker at conferences but still teaches the course to select businesses, public utilities agencies, medical and educational institutions throughout the world.

Michael has been a resident of Murrieta, CA for over 20 years and has developed lifelong relationships within the security community. He is extremely passionate about educating people to have a situational awareness mindset.

Learn more about Michael's other companies **National Business Investigations, Inc.** at **www.Investigations-NBI.com** and **MPS Security & Protection** at www.Security-MPS.com.

A.L.I.V.E.
833-99-ALIVE (25483)
www.ActiveShooterSurvivalTraining.com

ACTIVESHOOTERSURVIVALTRAINING.COM
833-99-ALIVE (25483)

Made in the USA
Columbia, SC
25 May 2023

17096186R00117